RAMAYANA

The Epic Retold for the Modern Reader

RAMAYANA

The Epic Retold for the Modern Reader

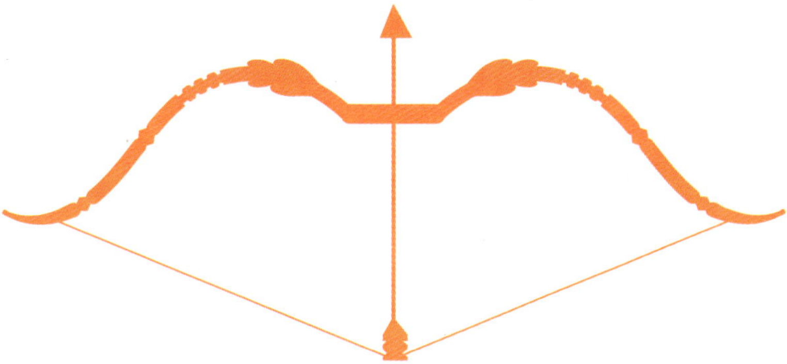

Nityanand Charan Das

EBD
EMBASSY BOOKS
www.embassybooks.in

First Indian Edition,

Published in 2026 by:

Embassy Book Distributors

120, Great Western Building, Maharashtra Chamber of

Commerce Lane, Fort, Mumbai 400 023, India

Email: info@embassybooks.in

www.embassybooks.in

EMBASSY BOOKS
www.embassybooks.in

P-ISBN: 978-81-19727-76-6

HB-ISBN: 978-81-19727-91-9

E-ISBN: 978-81-19727-98-8

Distribution Centres:

Mumbai, Ahmedabad, Bangalore, Kolkata, Chennai, Hyderabad, New Delhi, Pune

Cover and Layout Design by Rishikumar Thakur for Embassy Book Distributors

Cover & Inside Illustrations by Onkar Fondekar

Printed and bound in India by Thomson Press India Private Limited

TABLE OF CONTENT

Introduction
The Journey Begins

Long, long ago, in a golden kingdom called Ayodhya, lived a prince named Ram.

He wasn't just strong like a warrior or wise like a scholar—He was also kind, gentle, truthful, and full of love. He cared for everyone, whether they were kings or monkeys, sages or strangers. But more than anything, Ram always chose what was right, even when it was hard.

His story is not just about battles and palaces, forests and demons. It is about a son who listened to His parents, a brother who never left His side, a husband who loved with all His heart, and a king who ruled with justice and compassion.

This is the story of Ram—as told in the sacred *Ramayana*, written thousands of years ago by the great sage Valmiki. It has been sung and retold in temples and homes for generations, passed down like a treasure wrapped in love.

Now, this book brings that same treasure to you.

Each chapter has been lovingly retold so that the modern reader like yourself can read, enjoy, and understand it. You'll find wonder, adventure, friendship, and wisdom in every part of Ram's journey. You'll meet noble Ram, gentle Sita, brave Lakshman, mighty Hanuman, kind-hearted Bharat, and many others who lived for truth and love.

But remember—this is not just a story.

It is a path.

A path that teaches us how to live with courage, kindness, and honour.

A path that shows us how to be brave when we're afraid, how to stand by what's right, and how to love with all our heart.

A path that helps us become the very best version of ourselves.

Just like Ram.

So, take your first step into the forest of wonders.

The birds are singing. The wind is calling. The divine story is ready to unfold...

1

THE WISH OF A KING

A long time ago, in the heart of a beautiful land, there was a golden city called Ayodhya. It sparkled like a jewel on the banks of the sacred river Sarayu. The streets were clean and wide, the houses were grand, and the people were always smiling. Birds sang in lush green gardens, and the air was sweet with the scent of blooming flowers.

Ayodhya was ruled by a wise and noble king named Dashrath. He belonged to the glorious Ikshvaku dynasty and was known far and wide for his courage and kindness. He cared for his people like a loving father, and in return, they loved him dearly. Under his rule, there was peace and happiness. The rain always came at the right time, the crops grew rich and full, and no one in the kingdom ever went hungry. There were no thieves, no diseases, and no one ever told a lie.

But even in this perfect land, the great King Dashrath was not truly happy. His heart was heavy with one deep sorrow—he had no children. Day and night, he wished for a son who would grow up to rule Ayodhya with *dharma*, just as he had done.

One day, the wise royal priest, Sage Vasishtha, saw the king's sadness and said, "O King, do not worry. There is a special fire ritual called the *Putrakameshti Yajna*, which is meant for those who desire children. Invite the great Sage Rishyasringa to perform it. He is blessed with great spiritual power. With faith and devotion, your wish shall come true."

King Dashrath's eyes lit up with hope. He immediately sent his trusted ministers to the kingdom of Anga, where Sage Rishyasringa lived under the care of King Romapada, a close friend of Dashrath.

Sage Rishyasringa was not like others. He had grown up in a forest, far away from cities and people, raised by his father in complete simplicity and purity. In fact, he had never even seen a woman until he was once brought to the city of Anga to end a terrible drought. Just by his presence and his inner purity, the rains poured down and the kingdom flourished again. Later, Sage Rishyasringa married the daughter of King Romapada.

Now, hearing King Dashrath's request, Sage Rishyasringa agreed to come to Ayodhya with his wife. When they arrived, the people welcomed them with great honour, and preparations for the sacred *yajna* began at once.

The ritual was performed with utmost devotion. Sacred fires were lit, Vedic *mantras* were chanted, and *ghee* and offerings were poured into the flames. Sages and priests from across the land gathered, and the air was filled with holiness.

At that very moment, the heavenly gods were holding a secret

meeting. They were troubled by the demon king Ravana, who was spreading fear and destruction everywhere. Because of a boon he had received, Ravana could not be killed by heavenly gods, demons, or spirits. But in his arrogance, he had forgotten to ask protection from humans.

The heavenly gods turned to Lord Vishnu, the protector of the universe. "Only you can stop Ravana," they pleaded. "Please take birth on Earth as a human."

Lord Vishnu smiled. "Do not worry," He said. "I will be born as the son of King Dashrath."

Back at the *yajna*, something miraculous happened. From the sacred fire arose a shining, golden figure. He held a beautiful bowl in his hands, filled with a glowing sweet pudding called *payasa*, made of milk and rice.

He said gently, "O King Dashrath, this is a gift from the gods. Share it with your queens. You will soon be blessed with sons."

King Dashrath bowed with folded hands and deep gratitude. With great care, he divided the divine pudding. He gave half to his eldest queen, Kausalya, one quarter to Queen Kaikeyi, and the final quarter—split in two equal parts—to Queen Sumitra.

Time passed, and the palace of Ayodhya was filled with joy and celebration. Queen Kausalya gave birth to a radiant baby boy named Ram. Queen Kaikeyi gave birth to Bharat. Queen Sumitra gave birth to twin sons—Lakshman and Shatrughna.

All of Ayodhya rejoiced! People danced in the streets, music filled the air, and lights sparkled like stars. The gods smiled from above, and even the Earth seemed to sing with joy.

For Lord Vishnu had come to Earth—born as the noble Ram, the hero who would one day change the world.

2

THE FOUR PRINCES OF AYODHYA

The palace of Ayodhya was now filled with laughter, the gentle cries of babies, and the sweet songs of joy. Queen Kausalya gently held little Ram in her arms. His face glowed like the morning sun, and His eyes sparkled with wisdom far beyond His age. Everyone who saw Him felt peaceful and happy, as if the whole world had become brighter.

Queen Kaikeyi lovingly cradled her son Bharat, who had a noble gaze and a heart full of grace. Queen Sumitra had double the joy, for she had given birth to twin sons—Lakshman and Shatrughna—both full of life, charm, and strength.

The four brothers grew up together, just like the four petals of a blooming lotus. Ram was the eldest and most beloved. He was calm, gentle, and always truthful. From the time He could speak, He cared deeply for others. Lakshman loved Ram more than anything and followed Him everywhere like a shadow. Bharat and Shatrughna were just as close, always playing, learning, and laughing together.

King Dashrath watched his sons grow with pride and joy. He called for the best teachers in the land to educate them. The princes learned the Vedas and scriptures, archery and swordplay, music and philosophy. Ram learned everything quickly and with great focus. He was the favourite of not only the people of Ayodhya but also of all the sages and ministers who visited the royal court.

As the boys grew into young men, their virtues began to shine. Ram was brave but humble, strong but gentle. He protected the weak, respected the elders, and spoke kindly to all. His bow never missed its mark, and His wisdom never failed. Lakshman was always by His side—His loyal brother, ready to serve and protect Him at every step. Bharat was noble and just, and Shatrughna, though the youngest, was full of valour and always close to Bharat.

The people of Ayodhya would often gather outside the palace just to get a glimpse of the four brothers. "Ram is like the moon that cools the heart," they would say. "With such princes, our future is in safe hands."

But far away from the peaceful city, in a dark forest, something else was stirring.

A powerful sage named Vishwamitra, who had once been a great king himself, was performing deep penance and *yajnas* to please the gods. But his sacred rituals were being disturbed—terrible demons would appear and destroy everything, throwing bones and blood into the holy fires and scaring the sages away.

Vishwamitra, though mighty and wise, knew that to complete his *yajnas* peacefully, he needed a protector. Accordingly, he made up his mind and set out on a journey to the city of Ayodhya. He was going to ask King Dashrath for help. But not just any help—he wanted young Ram to come with him.

Would the king agree? Would the young prince leave His home to fight fierce demons in the forest?

The story of Ram's adventures was just beginning…

3

THE SAGE WITH A MISSION

One fine morning in Ayodhya, King Dashrath was seated on his grand throne in the royal court. Ministers, priests, and noblemen had gathered. Suddenly, a hush fell over the room. The guards bowed deeply, and the great sage Vishwamitra entered, glowing with spiritual power. His hair was matted, his eyes calm like a still lake, and his footsteps echoed with purpose.

King Dashrath immediately stood up and welcomed the sage with folded hands. "O Mighty One," he said, "your visit brings great honour to my kingdom. Please tell me how I may serve you."

Vishwamitra smiled gently and spoke, "O King, I am performing sacred *yajnas* in the forest to please the gods. But evil demons are disturbing the rituals. They throw bones and blood into the fire and scare the sages away. I need someone brave and pure-hearted to protect my *yajna*."

The king, having heard his plea, nodded. "Say the word, O

Sage, and I will send my armies."

But Vishwamitra shook his head. "I do not want an army. I want your son—Ram."

Hearing this, King Dashrath's heart skipped a beat. "Ram? He is just a boy! He has never been away from the palace. The forest is full of dangers. Let me come instead, or send my warriors. But not Ram… please, please ask for anything else."

But Vishwamitra was firm. "O King," he said, his voice calm but powerful, "do not doubt your son. Ram is no ordinary child. He is destined for greatness. He will be safe under my guidance. Trust in *dharma*. Trust in your son."

The king was torn. His heart was a storm of love and fear. But just then, the wise royal priest Sage Vasishtha stood up and said, "O King, Vishwamitra is no ordinary sage. If he has asked for Ram, there is a divine purpose. Let Ram go. The world will sing of His deeds for ages to come."

Hearing these words, Dashrath slowly agreed. With heavy eyes but a faithful heart, he called Ram and told Him everything.

Ram, shining like the sun, smiled and bowed at His father's feet. "Father, it is My duty and joy to protect the sages and uphold *dharma*. I will go."

Lakshman, who loved Ram more than life itself, stepped forward and said, "Where Ram goes, I shall go. I will never leave His side."

And so, the two brothers, dressed in simple clothes and carrying their bows and arrows, walked beside the powerful

Sage Vishwamitra. The people of Ayodhya stood silently as their beloved princes left the palace. Mothers whispered prayers. Flowers were offered to the sky.

The journey into the forests had begun. Ahead waited demons, mysteries, magical weapons, and the beginning of a story that would live forever.

4

RAM'S FIRST BATTLE—THE DEMONESS TATAKA

The forest was thick and wild. Giant trees whispered secrets to each other, and strange birds called out from the branches. Ram and Lakshman walked fearlessly, their bows in hand and quivers full of sharp arrows. Sage Vishwamitra led the way, his voice soft as he told them stories of ancient kings and mighty battles.

After walking for some time, the sage paused and pointed toward a dark and eerie part of the forest. "This is the dreadful land of Tataka," he said. "Long ago, she was a beautiful woman. But because of her evil actions and a curse, she turned into a terrible demoness. Now, she attacks sages, destroys *yajnas*, and eats anyone who enters her forest."

Lakshman's eyes flashed with anger. "How dare she disturb the peace of sages!" he said.

Ram remained calm but alert. "What must I do, O Sage?" he asked.

Vishwamitra looked at Ram with deep trust. "You must slay

Tataka. Only you have the strength and purity to stop her wickedness."

Ram hesitated for a moment. "But she is a woman. Is it right to raise My weapon against her?"

Sage Vishwamitra nodded solemnly. "True *dharma* is not about outer forms. When someone harms the innocent and blocks the path of goodness, they must be stopped—man or woman. Your duty is to protect the righteous."

Hearing these words, Ram strung His mighty bow. The sound echoed through the forest like thunder. Animals fled. The wind paused. Even the trees seemed to shiver.

Suddenly, a terrible roar shook the sky. Trees snapped, and the ground trembled. Out of the shadows came Tataka, a giant demoness with blazing eyes, wild hair, and sharp claws. She rushed toward them with terrifying speed.

Ram stood His ground. He placed an arrow on His bow and shot it with divine precision. It whizzed through the air and struck Tataka. She roared in pain and fury, vanishing into the forest and then appearing again from another side. She tried to confuse Him, throwing boulders and creating storms with her magic.

But Ram was steady. Arrow after arrow flew from His bow, glowing like lightning. Lakshman stood nearby, ready to help, but Ram faced Tataka alone. With one final, powerful shot, He released an arrow that struck her heart.

With a scream that echoed across the skies, Tataka fell to the ground, her giant body shaking the earth. The forest sighed in relief. Birds returned to their nests, and the sun shone once again.

Sage Vishwamitra's face lit up with joy. "Ram," he said, "You have done a great deed. You have freed this land from fear. Now, the sages can continue their *yajnas* in peace."

The sky rained flowers. Invisible beings sang praises. Ram's first battle was over, and the whole world seemed to celebrate.

But this was only the beginning.

5

RAM RECEIVES DIVINE WEAPONS

After the fearsome demoness Tataka was defeated, peace returned to the forest. The trees looked brighter, the birds sang sweeter, and the air itself seemed to smile. Sage Vishwamitra was very pleased with Ram and Lakshman.

The next morning, as golden sunlight streamed through the trees, Sage Vishwamitra called Ram and Lakshman to his side. His eyes sparkled like stars.

"O Ram," he said, "You have proven Yourself as a protector of *dharma*. Now I will give You gifts—no ordinary gifts, but divine weapons blessed by the gods themselves!"

Ram and Lakshman bowed with folded hands, their hearts full of respect.

Then, with powerful *mantras* (chants) and deep concentration, Sage Vishwamitra called forth the celestial weapons. One by one, they appeared before Ram like shining beings made of light.

There was *Shiv Dhanush*, a mighty bow with endless power.

There was *Brahmastra*, a flaming arrow that could destroy even the strongest enemy.

There was *Agneya*, a weapon born of fire, and *Vayavya*, which brought the force of the wind.

Varunastra sparkled with the might of the ocean, and *Parjanyastra* rumbled like thunderclouds.

Weapon after weapon—some shaped like serpents, some glowing like suns, some whispering secrets of the stars—came before Ram. There were weapons to freeze, to burn, to confuse, to protect, and to guide.

Sage Vishwamitra gave Ram the secret *mantras* to control each of them. Ram listened carefully, memorising every syllable with devotion. He promised to use them only for protecting the good and punishing the wicked.

Lakshman watched with wonder and pride. Though the weapons were given to Ram, he felt as if the strength of *dharma* itself was growing before his eyes.

The sage smiled. "Ram," he said, "You are now ready for anything that may come Your way."

Just then, the forest breeze picked up, and the leaves danced with joy. The earth itself seemed to bow before the divine prince.

With the blessings of the sage, the brothers continued their journey, now armed with powers beyond imagination—but still as humble and kind as ever.

Ahead waited deeper adventures: fearsome demons, royal festivals, and a princess whose beauty was matched only by her virtue.

But for now, the forest was quiet, and the stars twinkled above, as if they too had become Ram's protectors.

6

RAM PROTECTS THE SACRED *YAJNA*

The forest was peaceful once more, but Sage Vishwamitra had not yet completed his mission. There was still a great *yajna* to be performed—a sacred fire ceremony to please the gods and protect the world.

With Ram and Lakshman by his side, the sage reached a quiet, holy spot. It was surrounded by flowering trees, singing birds, and gentle winds. There, he began to prepare for the sacred rites, lighting the fire and chanting Vedic *mantras*. Sages from many places gathered to witness the powerful *yajna*.

But danger lurked in the skies.

Far away, in a dark part of the world, there lived two terrible demons—Maricha and Subahu. They were followers of the wicked Ravana and had only one goal: to ruin the holy *yajnas* of the sages. Whenever the sages chanted *mantras*, the demons would fly through the air and throw bones, blood, and filth into the fire, destroying everything.

They had tried many times before—and always succeeded. But

this time, something was different.

Ram was here.

Sage Vishwamitra sat before the fire, chanting *mantras*. "The *yajna* has begun," he said. "O Ram, be watchful. The demons may attack at any moment."

Ram stood guard, His bow ready and His eyes sharp. Lakshman stood beside Him, eager to help.

Suddenly, as the *yajna* neared completion, the skies turned black. Thunder cracked. Winds howled. A foul smell filled the air.

From the dark clouds above, two monstrous figures came flying—Maricha, tall as a mountain, and Subahu, covered in fire and smoke. They roared like wild beasts and began to hurl burning rocks, blood, and bones down at the sacred fire.

But this time, they were met with something unexpected: the calm strength of Ram.

With a steady hand, Ram picked up a blazing arrow blessed by the gods. He chanted a divine *mantra*, aimed carefully, and released it. The arrow soared through the sky like lightning and struck Maricha in the chest. But it did not kill him. Instead, it hurled him far, far away—across the ocean, deep into the wilderness. Maricha landed with a crash, terrified and defeated.

Next, Ram turned to Subahu. Another arrow propelled from His bow, sharp and bright like the sun. It struck the demon with such force that Subahu was destroyed on the spot, and eventually so were the other demons that had followed him.

The sky cleared. The winds calmed. The fire blazed brighter than ever.

The sages watched in awe. For the first time in many years, their *yajna* was completed without any disturbance. They showered blessings upon Ram. Flowers fell from the heavens. The earth seemed to glow with happiness.

Sage Vishwamitra smiled. "Ram," he said, "You have protected *dharma*. You are not just a prince—You are a hero chosen by the gods themselves."

Lakshman looked at his brother with pride, and the sages sang praises late into the night.

Thus ended the threat of the demons, and thus began the growing glory of Ram.

7

THE JOURNEY TO MITHILA— THE LAND OF SITA

With the demons defeated and the sacred *yajna* complete, the forest once again became a place of peace and song. Sage Vishwamitra's heart was full of joy and gratitude. But he had one more divine plan—a journey to a kingdom called Mithila, where a great event was about to take place.

"O Ram, O Lakshman," the sage said one morning, "let us now travel to Mithila. There, King Janak is holding a grand assembly. He has promised the hand of his daughter Sita to whoever can lift and string the mighty bow of Lord Shiva. No one on Earth has ever done it. Come, let us see this wondrous event."

Ram and Lakshman bowed. The name of Sita touched something deep in Ram's heart, though He had never met her.

As the journey to Mithila began, they passed through villages and forests, crossing rivers and hills. Everywhere they went, people came running to see the two radiant princes. Children smiled, old men blessed them, and the women whispered, "Surely, these boys are gods in human form."

One morning, as they walked through a peaceful grove, Sage

Vishwamitra stopped. Before them stood a silent hermitage. Its walls were overgrown with vines, and the air felt still, almost magical.

"This," said the sage quietly, "is the ashram of the great sage Gautama. Long ago, his wife Ahalya lived here."

Ram and Lakshman listened carefully as Vishwamitra told the story.

Ahalya had been a woman of unmatched beauty and devotion. But once, the king of the gods, Indra, came in disguise and tricked her. Sage Gautama, seeing what had happened, was filled with sorrow and cursed Ahalya to become invisible, her form hidden from the world. "You will remain unseen," he had said, "until the touch of Ram's feet restores you."

Sage Vishwamitra looked at Ram. "O Noble Prince, free her."

With quiet steps, Ram entered the ashram. As soon as His foot touched the ground, a soft glow rose from the earth. From that light emerged Ahalya—shining, purified, and full of devotion.

Falling at Ram's feet with tears in her eyes, she said, "O Lord, You have saved me."

The gods in the sky rejoiced. Flowers rained from above. Sage Gautama appeared and, seeing his wife restored and purified, welcomed her back with forgiveness and joy.

The forest once again blessed by their reunion, Ram, Lakshman, and Vishwamitra continued their journey.

After several days, the towers of Mithila rose in the distance—golden domes, tall gates, and sweet-smelling gardens. The city

sparkled with joy and celebration. Drums and flutes filled the air, garlands hung from every door, and people from all over the land had gathered for the great bow ceremony.

Sage Vishwamitra led Ram and Lakshman to the palace of King Janak. The king welcomed the sage with honour, folding his hands and offering a seat of respect.

When his eyes fell upon Ram, King Janak was amazed. "Who is this shining young prince?" he asked. "He walks like a lion, and His face glows like the moon."

Sage Vishwamitra replied with a smile, "This is Ram, the son of King Dashrath. He is full of virtue, strength, and divine grace. He has come to see your sacred bow."

King Janak's heart skipped a beat. "The bow of Shiva is heavy beyond measure. Many kings have tried to lift it—but none could even move it. If your prince can string it, then surely He is sent by the heavenly gods!"

That evening, as the sun dipped below the sky, Ram and Lakshman were taken to the royal gardens. There, walking among lotus ponds and mango trees, Ram heard the gentle name "Sita" spoken by the breeze.

And in another corner of the palace, Princess Sita, with eyes like lotus petals, stood at her window. Her heart stirred without knowing why.

Though they had not yet seen each other, their souls had already begun to remember a love older than time.

8

RAM STRINGS THE DIVINE BOW

The city of Mithila buzzed with excitement. Today was the day!

The grand bow ceremony was about to begin. In the royal hall, kings and princes from faraway lands had gathered, their crowns shining and their eyes fixed on one goal—to marry the beautiful Princess Sita. But her father, King Janak, had kept a condition: "Sita will only marry the one who can lift and string the mighty bow of Lord Shiva."

The royal court was decorated with silken canopies, golden lamps, and flower garlands. The sacred bow rested on a grand platform, heavy and tall, mounted on eight iron wheels. It was so powerful that even strong warriors couldn't move it an inch.

One by one, proud kings stepped forward. Muscles flexed, sweat dripped—but the bow did not budge.

Some pushed, some pulled, some even roared with anger. But nothing worked.

Then, Sage Vishwamitra turned quietly toward Ram and, without giving a command, softly said, "Dear Ram, behold the bow."

His eyes sparkled with deeper meaning—this was no ordinary request. Ram understood. The sage was not just pointing to the bow—he was signalling that the time had come. The time to act.

Ram stepped forward.

The hall fell silent.

Sita, watching from a balcony, held her breath. Her heart began to beat faster, though she did not understand why.

Ram walked with calm steps towards the bow. He bowed to the sages, to King Janak, to the bow and then offered prayers to Lord Shiva. With grace and ease, He reached out and placed His hand on the bow.

To everyone's astonishment, the bow moved—just like that!

With one smooth motion, Ram lifted it high above His head.

Gasps filled the air.

He bent the bow to string it—when suddenly… CRACK!

The bow broke in half with a thunderous sound that shook the Earth and echoed across the skies! The kings covered their ears. The animals ran. Even the gods looked down in amazement.

Sita's eyes filled with tears—not of fear, but of deep joy. A garland of fresh flowers slipped from her hands.

King Janak stood up, his voice filled with wonder. "This prince is no ordinary man. He is a treasure of *dharma* and strength! Sita is now truly His."

Sage Vishwamitra smiled, and Lakshman's face beamed with pride.

Thus, with one act of divine strength, Ram won the hand of Sita.

But this was not just a victory of power—it was the beginning of a sacred love, a union written by destiny.

Soon, messengers were sent to Ayodhya with the joyful news. King Dashrath and his royal family would soon arrive to celebrate the holy wedding.

9

THE WEDDING OF RAM AND SITA

The news of Ram breaking the great bow of Lord Shiva travelled like the wind. Birds carried it in the skies, sages spoke of it in forests, and the people of Ayodhya danced with joy.

In King Dashrath's court, the messengers bowed low and said, "O Great King, your son Ram has lifted and broken the bow of Shiva! King Janak has promised Princess Sita to Him in marriage. He requests your presence in Mithila."

Tears of happiness filled King Dashrath's eyes. "Prepare the chariots," he declared. "Let us go to Mithila at once!"

With grand fanfare, King Dashrath and his royal sons—Bharat and Shatrughna—rode in golden chariots. The streets were filled with song. People waved flags and flowers. The princes looked like gods descending from the heavens.

Meanwhile in Mithila, the palace was glowing with preparations. Princess Sita, dressed in a beautiful red silk saree, sat quietly in her chamber, her heart full of sweetness and devotion. Her friends sang wedding songs and decorated her hands with fragrant sandalwood and bright red *alta* (the ceremonial red dye).

Ram too was dressed in royal clothes—His dark, lotus-like eyes sparkled like stars, and a gentle smile danced on His lips. He seemed calm, but in His heart, He knew: this was no ordinary marriage—it was the meeting of two eternal souls.

Finally, the auspicious moment arrived. The sacred fire was lit. The sages chanted *mantras* that filled the sky with blessings.

Ram and Sita entered the wedding hall, their eyes meeting for the first time. It was as if the moon had found her sun, and the sky itself held its breath.

As the priests recited the holy verses, Sita placed a garland of flowers around Ram's neck. Ram then placed His garland gently on her. They circled the sacred fire seven times, their hearts united in love, duty, and *dharma*.

The gods showered flowers from the heavens. Celestial drums echoed in joy.

But the joy did not stop there! King Janak had another surprise. "My brother has a daughter named Urmila," he said. "Let her be wed to Lakshman!"

And so it was. Bharat married Mandavi, and Shatrughna married Shrutakirti—two more princesses of Mithila.

Four sacred weddings, four noble princes, four graceful brides.

All of Mithila and Ayodhya rejoiced as if the entire universe had become a garden of happiness.

Ram and Sita sat together, not just as prince and princess, but as the embodiment of *dharma* and love—two hearts who would walk the path of life side by side, come joy or sorrow.

10

THE JOYFUL RETURN TO AYODHYA

The city of Mithila was filled with laughter, music, and celebration.

Four royal weddings had taken place, and hearts were overflowing with joy. But now it was time for the princes and their brides to return to Ayodhya.

King Dashrath, along with King Janak and the royal families, prepared for the grand journey. Chariots were decorated with golden bells, silk canopies, and flower garlands. The streets of Mithila were lined with smiling people who waved and threw petals as the royal procession set out.

As they crossed into the kingdom of Kosala, something magical happened. The trees bowed with joy. Rivers sparkled brighter. Even the animals seemed to dance. Mother Earth herself felt blessed to have Ram and Sita walk upon her.

But just then, the sky darkened slightly. The wind grew still. A powerful presence was approaching. The sages sensed it. The earth trembled ever so lightly.

Suddenly, from the forest emerged a tall figure with matted locks and eyes blazing like fire. He held a great axe in one hand and a mighty bow in the other. It was none other than Parashuram—the warrior-sage and sixth avatar of Lord Vishnu—famous for having rid the earth of corrupt *kshatriyas* twenty-one times.

All stood still. Parashuram's gaze was fixed upon Ram.

He thundered, "I have heard that You broke the bow of Lord Shiva. That bow belonged to my Lord! Do You think You are strong enough to handle the bow of Vishnu?"

He planted Vishnu's own bow on the ground and challenged Ram: "If You are truly worthy, string this divine bow and shoot an arrow from it. Only then will I believe You are not an arrogant prince."

The crowd gasped. Even King Dashrath grew worried, trembling at the fierce energy of Parashuram.

But Ram, calm and composed, stepped forward. With folded hands, He said respectfully, "O Great One, I have no pride. I simply followed the command of My *guru* and lifted the bow at King Janak's court. But if it pleases you, I shall try to string this bow as well."

With perfect ease and humility, Ram picked up the heavy bow of Vishnu. In a single movement, He strung it and placed an arrow upon it.

At that moment, the power of Lord Vishnu radiated from Him.

Ram said, "O Parashuram, now that the bow is strung and the arrow fixed, I cannot take it back without releasing it. Tell Me, O Noble Sage, where shall I aim this arrow?"

Parashuram's eyes widened. He had a sudden realisation—this was no ordinary prince. He was face-to-face with the very incarnation of the Lord he worshipped.

He bowed low and said, "O Ram, I now see that You are the Supreme Being Himself. Please direct Your arrow to destroy the fruits of my penance, so that my pride may also be removed."

Ram released the arrow, and the winds swirled as it blazed into the horizon, burning away Parashuram's spiritual burden and ego.

Parashuram folded his hands in deep reverence and said, "May You be victorious in all You do, O Lord." He then disappeared into the forest, his heart now humbled and at peace.

The procession resumed its journey.

When the grand procession neared Ayodhya, the city lit up like never before. Trumpets and conch shells sounded from every corner. The people of Ayodhya had waited with eager hearts to see their beloved prince again.

"Ram is coming! Ram is coming!" the children shouted.

"Sita, the princess of Mithila, will be our queen!" the women whispered with joy.

The palace gates were opened wide, and the royal chariots rolled in. Queen Kausalya, Queen Kaikeyi, and Queen Sumitra ran to embrace their sons and daughters-in-law. Tears of love filled their eyes.

Flowers rained from balconies, and the streets were covered in fragrant petals. The entire city was decorated with oil lamps, colourful flags, and sacred symbols drawn with rice flour.

That night, the palace echoed with music and song. The people danced, the sages blessed the newlyweds, and even the stars above seemed to shine a little brighter.

Ram and Sita stood at the palace balcony, looking at their people with deep love. They knew their journey was only beginning, but for now, their hearts were full.

Ayodhya was once again filled with peace, prosperity, and happiness—for *dharma* had returned home.

11

THE EVIL PLANS OF QUEEN KAIKEYI

Ayodhya shone like heaven on earth. The people were full of joy, the skies rained blessings, and King Dashrath's heart overflowed with happiness. He decided it was time to crown Ram as the next king.

Early one morning, in the royal court, he declared, "Ram shall be *Yuvaraja*—the Crown Prince of Ayodhya! He is brave, wise, and beloved by all." Everyone rejoiced. This was the moment everyone had been waiting for.

The news spread like a festival wind. People decorated their homes, cows were painted with turmeric, and sweet dishes were prepared. Everywhere you looked, there were lamps, flowers, and smiling faces. People sang and danced with joy.

But not everyone was happy.

Queen Kaikeyi, the youngest of Dashrath's three queens, heard the news from her maid Manthara. Manthara, with a heart full of jealousy, hissed, "If Ram becomes king, your son Bharat will be nothing! Don't let this happen!"

At first, Kaikeyi was surprised. "But Ram is like a son to me," she said.

However, Manthara kept whispering bitter words, twisting Kaikeyi's thoughts. Like a drop of poison in sweet milk, her heart turned hard. Due to the bad influence of the envious Manthara, Kaikeyi eventually agreed to execute an evil plan.

After listening to the wicked counsel of Manthara, Queen Kaikeyi did not go to the royal celebration. Instead, she entered the *kopabhavan*—the chamber of anger—where queens would go when displeased. She removed her ornaments, let her hair loose, and lay down on the bare floor in sorrowful silence.

King Dashrath, filled with joy from the preparations for Ram's coronation, came to Kaikeyi's palace to share the news with his beloved queen. He had always cherished her the most. He entered with a smile, expecting her to rejoice.

But as he stepped inside, he saw Kaikeyi lying on the cold floor, her jewellery cast aside, her face dark with sorrow.

Alarmed, he rushed to her side. "My beloved queen," he said, "what is the matter? Who has wronged you? Ask anything of me—I swear by Ram, ask for even the impossible, and I shall grant it."

Kaikeyi sat up slowly. Her face was stern, her voice cold. "You speak of promises," she said. "Do you remember the two boons you once granted me when I saved your life in battle against the enemies?"

King Dashrath, without suspecting anything, replied, "Yes, of course. Ask anything, my queen. Even if it costs me my life, I shall give it."

Kaikeyi's eyes blazed. "Then listen, O King. For my first boon, I ask that my son Bharat be made the Crown Prince of Ayodhya. And for the second—I ask that Ram be banished to the forest for fourteen years. He must not wear royal clothes. He must live like an ascetic, in the robes of bark, dwelling among the trees."

King Dashrath froze. It felt like thunder had struck his heart.

"What... what are you saying?" he gasped. "Ram is my life! Without Him, I cannot breathe!"

But Kaikeyi stood firm, unmoved by his sorrow. "A promise is a promise," she said.

The king cried and pleaded. He fell to the floor, clutching his heart. But Kaikeyi remained like a wall of stone.

Outside, the city sang with joy, unaware that a storm had entered the palace.

Inside, King Dashrath lay broken, trapped by his own words.

The sun of Ayodhya was about to be hidden behind dark clouds.

But little did anyone know—Ram, the jewel of *dharma*, would shine brighter than ever, even in exile.

12

RAM ACCEPTS EXILE WITH A SMILE

Morning arrived in Ayodhya with drums and conch shells. People gathered in the streets wearing their finest clothes, ready to celebrate the crowning of Ram.

But inside the palace, there was silence. Heavy silence.

King Dashrath sat on his throne with eyes full of sorrow. His heart was broken, and his lips could not speak.

Ram, unaware of the storm, entered with a bright smile. He bowed to His father and said, “I have come, dear father. Please give your blessing. Why do you look so sad?”

But the king could not say a word.

Queen Kaikeyi stepped forward. Her voice was calm, but her words were sharp like thorns. “Ram, Your father has given me two promises. One—Bharat shall be king. Two—You must go to the forest for fourteen years.”

Not a trace of anger appeared on Ram’s face. His smile did not fade. His eyes did not burn with tears.

He folded His hands and said, "As you wish, Mother. I shall leave for the forest today."

Kaikeyi was stunned. She had expected shock or protest—but there was none.

Ram then bowed to His father. "Do not grieve, O King. A promise must be kept. I shall protect your word with My life."

Dashrath wept like a child. "Ram! I never wanted this! Forgive me!"

Ram gently held His father's hand. "A son's duty is to uphold his father's honour. I am proud to do so."

He walked calmly to His mother, Queen Kausalya, and told her everything.

Her heart shattered. "Why must You suffer, my child? You are the light of Ayodhya!"

But Ram held her close. "Mother, it is for *dharma*. The forest is now My kingdom, and trees My palace."

Sita, hearing this, said firmly, "Wherever You go, I go. I am Your wife. I belong with You—in joy or sorrow."

And Lakshman, ever loyal, said, "Brother, I too shall come. I will guard You like Your shadow."

That evening, the three of them—Ram, Sita, and Lakshman—dressed in simple bark clothes, left the palace.

The people of Ayodhya cried out, "No! Do not leave us!" But Ram smiled and blessed them all.

As they walked into the forest, the trees bowed, the wind whispered songs of praise, and even the animals watched with tearful eyes.

Thus began a new chapter of the divine journey—where royalty wore rags, and the forest became a stage for the greatest story of love, truth, and sacrifice.

13

BHARAT'S RETURN AND HIS PAINFUL DISCOVERY

Far away in his uncle's kingdom, young Prince Bharat was spending a peaceful time. But one night, he had a strange and troubling dream. It was filled with darkness, crying faces, and a broken throne.

Suddenly, a messenger arrived with urgent news: "Prince Bharat, your father, King Dashrath, has fallen very ill. You must return to Ayodhya at once."

Without delay, Bharat and his brother Shatrughna rode back with heavy hearts. As they entered Ayodhya, something felt terribly wrong.

The streets were silent.

No music.
No laughter.
No garlands.
No welcome.

It was as if the entire city was holding its breath.

Bharat rushed into the palace and cried out, "Where is Father? Where is my brother Ram? Why is Ayodhya so quiet?"

No one answered.

At last, Queen Kaikeyi came forward with a proud smile and said, "Rejoice, my son! Your father has fulfilled two promises to me. He made you king, and he sent Ram to the forest for fourteen years!"

Bharat's heart stopped. "What did you say?!"

Kaikeyi repeated the cruel tale with no shame.

Bharat was horrified. His eyes filled with tears and his voice trembled with pain. "I never wanted the throne! I would never take it by hurting Ram! You have done a terrible thing, Mother."

He ran to his father's chamber—but it was too late. King Dashrath had left his body, crying Ram's name with his final breath.

Bharat fell to the ground and wept. "O Father, why did you not wait for me? Why did you send Ram away?"

Shatrughna, filled with anger, caught the wicked maid Manthara and almost punished her, but Bharat stopped him.

"No. Just leave her. This pain must end not with anger, but with truth."

Bharat refused to wear the royal crown. He said before the whole court, "This kingdom belongs to Ram. I shall go to the forest and bring Him back!"

He took off his royal jewels, dressed in simple clothes, and gathered his army—not to conquer, but to serve.

With his heart full of love and sorrow, Bharat set out toward the forest. The people of Ayodhya followed him, hoping that soon their beloved Ram would return.

14

BHARAT MEETS RAM IN THE FOREST

Through forests deep and rivers wide, Bharat travelled with a heart full of hope and sorrow. Along with him came ministers, elders, soldiers, and villagers—all longing to see their beloved Ram again.

But the journey was not easy—not because of the terrain, but because of the sorrow in people's hearts.

As Bharat's vast procession moved through villages and hermitages, many sages, ascetics, and forest dwellers dealt with suspicion. They thought and expressed, "Here comes the prince who sent his brother into exile. Now he brings an army—does he plan to harm Ram?"

Some turned away in anger, others hid from sight. Even animals seemed to withdraw.

Seeing their reactions, Bharat felt a pain deeper than any wound. He stopped his chariot and addressed the crowd in many places.

"O Noble Ones," he said with folded hands, "do not mistake me. I did not ask for the kingdom. I did not send Ram away. These tears in my eyes are not of pride but of grief. I have come to fall at His feet and beg Him to return."

His voice, filled with truth and sorrow, melted the hearts of the listeners. Slowly, people began to believe him. Some cried. Some blessed him. Some even joined the journey.

After many days, they reached the *ashram* of Sage Bharadvaja. The sage welcomed Bharat and said, "I know why you've come. Your love for Ram is pure. Go to Chitrakuta. That is where He stays."

Bharat folded his hands. "Please bless me, O Sage. I only want to bring my brother back."

The next morning, the grand entourage journeyed to Chitrakuta, where the trees whispered softly and the mountain stood tall like a watchful friend.

Ram, Sita, and Lakshman had made a small hut of leaves and bark. Their days were peaceful—filled with prayers, caring for the forest, and listening to sages.

But that day, Lakshman saw dust rising in the distance. "Brother, a great army is coming! Could it be danger?"

Ram looked calmly and said, "Let us not be hasty. That is Bharat. I see no anger—only sorrow on his face."

Soon, Bharat arrived. The moment he saw Ram, he ran forward and fell at His feet.

He cried, "Brother! Please forgive me! I had no part in Mother Kaikeyi's wicked plans. I have come to bring You home! Father is no more!"

Grief-stricken to learn of King Dashrath's loss, Ram gently lifted Bharat and hugged him. "Dear brother, I know your heart. But I must obey Father's word. Fourteen years I shall stay in the forest. That is My duty."

The brothers wept, holding each other tightly.

Sita and Lakshman stood by with tears in their eyes.

Bharat begged again and again, "Please return, Ram! Ayodhya is like a night without the moon!"

But Ram's decision was firm. "A promise once made must never be broken."

Bharat understood. He placed Ram's wooden sandals on his head and said, "Then rule Ayodhya through these, O Lord. I shall guard Your kingdom as Your servant until You return."

He built a small cottage in Nandigram, outside Ayodhya, and placed the wooden sandals on the royal throne.

Every day, he ruled in Ram's name, wearing bark cloth and living simply, waiting for the day his beloved brother would return.

And thus, the forest echoed with the cries of love—not just from one brother to another, but from a whole kingdom to its true king.

15

MEETING THE GREAT SAGE ATRI AND ANASUYA

After Bharat left with Ram's sandals, the forest felt quiet once again. The sky above Chitrakuta was bright, but Ram, Sita, and Lakshman knew it was time to move on.

Ram said, "This forest may soon fill with people searching for us. Let us go deeper into the woods, where sages live and peace flows like a river."

So they journeyed onward—walking under the shade of tall trees, crossing streams where deer drank, and listening to birds that sang like temple bells.

At last, they reached the peaceful hermitage of the great sage Atri Muni.

Sage Atri was old and wise, with matted hair and eyes that sparkled with kindness. As soon as he saw Ram, he stood with folded hands and said, "Welcome, O Prince of Ayodhya! My heart is blessed to see You."

Ram bowed and replied, "O Great Sage, we have come to live

simply and learn from the holy ones like you."

Sita also offered her respects, and that is when she met a most divine and gentle lady—Anasuya, the sage's wife.

Anasuya was famous for her purity and devotion. With a soft smile, she welcomed Sita and said, "Come, dear child. You are a princess, yet you walk through the forest with joy. You are truly special."

Sita sat beside her, and the two spoke like a mother and daughter.

Anasuya lovingly said, "Sita, a wife's strength lies in her love, patience, and *dharma*. You are setting a noble example for all."

As a gift, Anasuya gave Sita beautiful clothes, fragrant oils, and divine ornaments that would never fade. "Wear these in the forest, dear one. Let them bring you comfort and courage."

Sita smiled and touched Anasuya's feet in gratitude.

After spending the night peacefully at Sage Atri's ashram, Ram, Sita, and Lakshman rose early the next morning. They offered respectful farewells to Sage Atri and Anasuya. With folded hands, Ram said, "O Revered Ones, your blessings are our greatest wealth. We now continue to the deeper forest, as we have promised to dwell in the wilderness." Anasuya embraced Sita like a mother, and the sages blessed them with words of protection. Thus, after receiving their blessings, the three travellers set off toward the Dandaka Forest.

They didn't know what dangers or wonders awaited them next.

But one thing was certain—their path was protected by the blessings of saints, and their hearts were full of love and courage.

16

ENTERING THE MYSTERIOUS DANDAKA FOREST

With the blessings of Sage Atri and Mother Anasuya shining in their hearts, Ram, Lakshman, and Sita walked deeper into the forest.

Soon, the trees grew taller, their branches twisted like arms reaching to the sky. Strange calls of animals echoed all around. This was the Dandaka Forest—a vast and wild place known for its fierce creatures, hidden sages, and… dangerous demons.

But Ram walked ahead fearlessly. Lakshman followed with his bow ready, while Sita walked beside them, her heart calm with faith in her Lord.

Suddenly, from between the dark trees, a figure appeared. It was a powerful, shining *rishi* named Sharabhanga. His matted hair glowed like silver fire, and his eyes were as calm as a quiet river.

"Welcome, Ram," he said with joy. "I have waited for You. The gods told me You would come."

Ram bowed. "O Sage, we seek to protect the sages and live a

life of *dharma*. Please guide us."

Sage Sharabhanga smiled. "You are the protector of righteousness, dear Ram. My time on Earth is over. I have waited only to see You."

Before their eyes, Sharabhanga sat in deep meditation. His body glowed like gold, and with divine light, he left the world, rising to the heavens in a beam of brilliance.

Ram, Lakshman, and Sita stood in awe, offering respect to the great sage.

They walked onward and met many more sages—some lived in small huts, others under trees. All were troubled.

One sage said, "Ram, the demons trouble our *yajnas*. They destroy our offerings and frighten us. Please protect us."

Ram's eyes shone with promise. "Fear not. I have come to uphold *dharma*. I shall protect you all."

And so, the forest, once filled with fear, now began to feel safe under the watch of the divine prince.

The birds chirped softly. The trees swayed gently. Even the wind seemed to whisper, "Ram has come."

But deep in the shadows, powerful demons were watching. They didn't yet know that their days of terror were coming to an end…

17

THE FIERCE ENCOUNTER WITH VIRADHA

As Ram, Sita, and Lakshman walked deeper into the wild Dandaka Forest, the trees became thicker and the air heavy. Strange growls and howls echoed all around. But Ram was calm. His bow was strong, and His heart even stronger.

Suddenly, the ground shook. Birds flew away in fear. From behind the trees burst a huge, terrifying figure. He had wild hair, blood-red eyes, and sharp yellow teeth. He roared like thunder.

"I am Viradha!" he bellowed. "I eat flesh and roam the forest freely. Who dares enter my land?"

Sita trembled, but stood bravely behind Ram. Lakshman stepped forward, anger blazing in his eyes.

Ram calmly said, "We are princes of Ayodhya. We follow *dharma* and harm no one. Let us pass in peace."

But Viradha laughed. "I want your golden princess! She will come with me!"

Before he could take a step, Lakshman shot a sharp arrow. It struck Viradha—but to their surprise, he did not fall. He pulled the arrow out and roared again!

Ram and Lakshman quickly drew more arrows and aimed carefully. Arrows flew like lightning, hitting Viradha's arms and legs. Yet the monster kept coming!

Then Ram remembered something. "Lakshman, he has a boon. Arrows cannot kill him. We must use our strength."

Together, the brothers dropped their bows and charged at Viradha. A fierce fight followed. Trees shook. Animals ran. Dust rose into the air.

With mighty power, Ram and Lakshman lifted the huge demon, wrestled him to the ground, and broke his arms. Viradha fell with a thud.

But he was still alive.

Ram then dug a deep pit in the earth with His own hands. With great effort, the brothers threw the demon into the pit and covered him with soil and stones.

At that moment, Viradha's face changed. The curse lifted. His monstrous form disappeared, and a shining celestial being rose from the ground.

He folded his hands and said, "Thank You, Lord Ram. Long ago, I was a heavenly being cursed to be a *rakshasa*. You have freed me. I can now return to the heavens."

And with that, he vanished in a beam of light.

The forest grew silent again.

Sita smiled with pride. Ram had once again protected the innocent and punished the wicked.

And the journey through the forest continued—toward more adventures and deeper truths.

18

THE GOLDEN HERMITAGE OF SUTIKSHNA MUNI

After the fierce battle with the demon Viradha, the forest felt calmer. The birds returned to their songs, and a gentle breeze rustled the leaves once again.

Ram, Sita, and Lakshman walked with steady steps through the green wilderness. Guided by *dharma* and devotion, they came to a peaceful ashram nestled beneath tall, graceful trees. The air was fragrant with flowers, birds chirped joyfully, and deer walked without fear. This was the hermitage of Sutikshna Muni, a noble and wise sage.

The sage, with matted hair and a glowing face, welcomed them warmly. "Ah, the divine princes of Ayodhya! And the noble Sita! The forest is blessed by your presence."

Ram and Lakshman bowed respectfully, and Sita offered a gentle *pranam*.

"O Sage," Ram said with folded hands, "We have come to protect the sages of this forest and to live the life of exile as per our father's vow. Kindly guide us."

Sage Sutikshna smiled, his eyes filled with wonder. "O Ram, You are the very Lord of *dharma*! We have long prayed for protection from the demons who disturb our sacred *yajnas*. Your presence is the answer to our prayers."

The sage offered them a seat and spoke gently: "Many hermitages lie ahead, deep within the Dandaka Forest. Great sages live there, performing *tapasya* and *yajnas*. They suffer from the attacks of cruel demons. Please visit them. They will bless You, and You can guard their sacred work."

Ram nodded with firm resolve. "I shall do all I can to protect them."

That night, the moon bathed the forest in a silvery glow. In Sage Sutikshna's peaceful *ashram*, birds slept in trees, and gentle animals lay close. Sita rested peacefully, Lakshman stood guard, and Ram sat under a tree in deep thought.

Though He was in exile, His heart was full—not of sorrow, but of purpose.

He was not just a prince now—He was a protector of the sages, the hope of the forest, and the upholder of righteousness.

With the blessings of Sage Sutikshna, the trio prepared to journey deeper into the sacred heart of the forest, where greater tests awaited.

19

SAGE AGASTYA AND THE DIVINE WEAPONS

The next morning, golden sunlight streamed through the tall trees. Birds sang sweetly as Ram, Sita, and Lakshman left the peaceful *ashram* of Sage Sutikshna and ventured deeper into the Dandaka Forest. Each step led them to places where the air was thick with ancient secrets and the ground whispered stories of sages and gods.

As they left, Sage Sutikshna had told them, "You must visit the *ashram* of the great Sage Agastya. He is no ordinary sage. He is famous throughout the three worlds for his wisdom and power."

After many days of journeying, they finally reached the *ashram* of Sage Agastya. The trees seemed to bow in reverence around his hermitage. A peaceful glow surrounded the place, and Ram immediately felt a deep sense of calm.

Sage Agastya, a short but mighty figure with glistening eyes, welcomed them with joy. "O Ram, I have been waiting for You. The gods had told me of Your arrival. You are the one who will destroy evil and protect *dharma*!"

Ram, Sita, and Lakshman offered their respectful obeisances. Then, the sage said something truly amazing.

"O Ram, the time has come for You to receive divine weapons. These are not ordinary weapons—they were once held by the gods themselves."

From a sacred spot, the sage brought out shining bows, quivers filled with endless arrows, and a powerful sword with a glowing hilt.

"This bow belonged to Lord Vishnu," he said with a smile. "These arrows will never miss their mark, and this sword shines with the fire of righteousness. Take them, Ram. Use them to protect the sages and destroy the wicked."

Ram accepted the weapons with folded hands, feeling their divine power flow through Him. Even Lakshman stood in awe.

Then, Agastya told them a story.

"Long ago," he said, "I drank up the ocean to punish a group of prideful demons. With the blessings of the gods, I helped restore peace. Now, O Ram, You must carry that same mission forward. Protect this forest. Punish the evil demons who trouble innocent sages."

Ram promised, "I shall not let a single *rakshasa* harm the sages. As long as I walk this forest, *dharma* shall be protected."

That evening, Ram and Lakshman sat beneath the stars, inspecting their new weapons. Sita watched them with love and admiration. She knew her Lord was no ordinary prince—He was a divine hero sent to bring peace to the world.

And so, armed with celestial weapons and a heart full of compassion, Ram continued His journey—not just through the forest, but into the hearts of all who would hear His glorious tale.

20

RAM VOWS TO PROTECT THE SAGES

With the blessings of Sage Agastya and the divine weapons in His hands, Ram walked with newfound strength through the vast and ancient Dandaka Forest. Sita followed close, her heart full of trust and love. Lakshman, ever alert, kept his eyes on every shadow and sound.

The forest was beautiful—but it was not peaceful.

Dark clouds of fear hovered over the hermitages of the sages. Ferocious demons, led by cruel leaders like Khara and Dushana, had been troubling them. These demons hated the sacred *yajnas* and disturbed the peace of the *rishis*. Some sages had even given up their rituals out of fear.

As Ram and His companions entered deeper into the forest, the sages came to greet them. Their eyes were filled with hope.

"O Noble Ram," they said, "we have been waiting for You. We are unable to do our *tapasya* in peace. The demons throw bones and blood into our fire offerings. They mock the Vedas and destroy our homes. Please protect us."

Ram's heart stirred with compassion and determination.

"These demons," He said firmly, "are enemies of *dharma*. How can I stay silent when sages who uphold truth and peace are suffering? I have taken a vow—I will protect every sage in this forest. As long as I live, no *rakshasa* shall harm you."

The sages were filled with joy. Their faces lit up with the hope of safety. Some wept with relief. Others blessed Ram with powerful *mantras* and offered Him fruit and water with trembling hands.

That night, sitting under the stars, Lakshman said, "Brother, Your words have brought courage back to the hearts of these sages. But the path ahead will be dangerous."

Ram smiled gently. "Lakshman, we are *kshatriyas*. It is our duty to protect those who live by truth. These forests may be dark, but we shall light them with righteousness."

Sita listened quietly. Though the dangers of the forest were many, she felt no fear. With Ram by her side, she knew only goodness could win.

Thus began a new chapter in the forest exile—not one of hiding or fear, but of standing tall, of protecting the helpless, and of restoring peace where evil had spread.

And in the heart of Dandaka, the demons began to feel a chill—for the protector of the sages, the warrior of *dharma*, had arrived.

21

THE WRATH OF SHURPANAKHA

Deep within the Dandaka Forest, where tall trees whispered secrets and wild animals roamed freely, lived a fearsome demoness named Shurpanakha. She was the sister of Ravana, the mighty demon king of Lanka. Shurpanakha was ugly in form and wicked in heart. She wandered the forest spreading fear and causing trouble for sages and travellers alike.

One day, as she was wandering through the forest looking for food and mischief, her sharp eyes spotted something unusual—a handsome young prince with strong arms and a gentle smile, walking through the woods with a beautiful princess and another brave-looking warrior.

It was Ram, Sita, and Lakshman.

Shurpanakha was stunned. "Who are these people?" she hissed. As she looked closer, her heart leapt. Ram's divine beauty enchanted her completely—she forgot that her own grotesque form was far from worthy of Him. She thought, *I must have this man as my husband!*

Changing her appearance into that of a beautiful woman, Shurpanakha approached Ram and said sweetly, "O Mighty Warrior, who are You? You look like a king but walk through the forest like a hermit. I am Shurpanakha, a demoness of great power. Marry me, and we shall rule this forest together!"

Ram smiled politely and said, "O Lady, I am already married. This is My dear wife, Sita. Perhaps you should speak to My younger brother Lakshman."

Instantly, Shurpanakha turned to Lakshman and made the same offer. But Lakshman laughed and said, "I am just a servant of my brother and have nothing of my own. Why would you want to marry me?"

Shurpanakha again returned to Ram with the proposal, but Ram refused her once more, gently reminding her of His commitment to Sita.

Shurpanakha's smile twisted into a terrible scowl. Her jealousy burst into flames when she looked at Sita. "She is the reason Ram refuses me!" she shrieked. "I will destroy her!"

In her fury, she rushed toward Sita, claws outstretched, ready to attack. But before she could come close, Lakshman, ever alert and protective, stepped forward like a blazing fire blocking a moth.

With swift precision, and in obedience to Ram's subtle command, Lakshman drew his sword and struck. In a flash, he sliced off her nose and ears. Blood poured from her face, and her shrieks echoed through the forest, wild and terrifying.

Bleeding and furious, she fled deep into the woods, her heart burning with revenge. "You will regret this!" she roared. "I will bring my brothers and destroy you all!"

Ram stood calmly, shielding Sita with His presence, while Lakshman remained alert and ready. The peaceful forest had now become a battleground for *dharma* and *adharma*.

Thus, the wicked demoness raced toward her brother's kingdom, setting into motion a chain of events that would change the world forever.

22

KHARA AND DUSHANA'S ATTACK

Shurpanakha raced through the forest like a storm. Her nose and ears were bleeding, her hair was wild, and her eyes blazed with fury. She flew straight to her brothers—Khara and Dushana, fierce commanders of Ravana's army who ruled a part of the forest with thousands of demons.

Wailing loudly, she cried, "Brothers! A human prince has insulted me! He cut off my nose and ears just because I wanted to marry Him! He lives in the forest with another man and a woman. You must take revenge for your sister!"

Khara's eyes turned red with rage. "No one dares insult my family! I will destroy this prince and His brother!" he thundered.

At once, Khara sent fourteen strong demons, each one fierce and powerful, to capture and kill Ram. They flew through the forest, roaring like thunderclouds.

But Ram was ready.

He gently told Sita, "Stay behind Me, dear one. No harm shall come to you. These demons have come to disturb the peace of the forest—I will stop them."

With His shining bow and divine arrows, Ram stood tall like a lion. As the demons charged at Him, Ram moved swiftly and gracefully. One by one, He struck them down. His arrows glowed like fire and flew faster than lightning.

Within moments, all fourteen demons lay defeated.

Back at the demon's camp, Shurpanakha screamed, "They are all dead! Khara, you must go yourself with your full army!"

Khara was furious. "I will go with Dushana and fourteen-thousand demons! We will crush this Ram into dust!"

The dark sky rumbled as the massive army marched toward Ram's cottage. Trees shook, animals ran, and even the sages felt fear.

But Ram remained calm. "Lakshman," He said, "take Sita to a safe cave nearby. Guard her well. Today I must fight alone."

Lakshman obeyed, though his heart longed to stay and help. From the hill, Sita and Lakshman watched as the forest below filled with fire and battle cries.

Ram stood alone—one man against thousands.

The earth shook. Arrows filled the sky. But Ram moved like a god of war. His divine weapons, gifted by sages and gods, whirled through the air. His bow sang with every shot. Demons fell like trees in a storm. Dushana charged at Ram with a roar—but was struck down. Khara himself fought fiercely—but Ram, with a final blazing arrow, brought him down too.

Silence fell over the battlefield. The forest breathed again.

The sages rejoiced. The birds sang once more. And Ram, the protector of *dharma*, returned to Sita and Lakshman, untouched, victorious, and humble.

But somewhere in Lanka, when Ravana would hear of Khara's defeat, his heart would burn with anger. He would now act—and the great war between good and evil would truly begin.

23

THE ABDUCTION OF SITA

Far away in the golden city of Lanka, the demon king Ravana sat on his magnificent throne. He was powerful, proud, and feared by all. But his pride was greater than his wisdom.

Shurpanakha entered his court with her face covered. Her voice trembled with anger.

"O Brother," she cried and spoke cunningly, "I was insulted and hurt by a prince in the forest. He cut off my nose and ears—all because I wished to bring a beautiful girl named Sita for you. His name is Ram. Sita is His wife and more beautiful than any goddess. If you truly love your sister, take revenge! Capture Sita and make her yours!"

Ravana's eyes narrowed. "Sita, more beautiful than the queens of heaven?" he whispered.

Filled with wicked desire and burning ego, he went to his uncle, the clever demon Maricha, who could take any form.

Maricha received Ravana with respect and suspicion. He had once been hurled across the ocean by a single arrow of Ram and had not forgotten the pain or power.

"Maricha," Ravana said, "I want your help. Disguise yourself as a golden deer and roam before Ram's hermitage. Sita will ask for it. Ram will chase you, and while He is away, I will take Sita."

Maricha, who had once been defeated by Ram's arrow, shivered.

"Do not do this, O King. I know Ram. He is no ordinary man. He is the Supreme Lord Himself. His arrows are like fire, and His wrath is death. I barely escaped Him once. If you force me to do this, know that I will surely die. But if you go ahead with your plan, you too will perish. Your kingdom will fall. Your family will be destroyed."

Ravana paused.

For a moment, Maricha's words struck like thunder in his mind. The fear of Ram began to stir in him. He clenched his fists and paced. His ego clashed with reason. Though obsessed with Sita, Ravana was not yet ready to risk his throne.

And so, for that time, he turned back.

Though Ravana returned to Lanka, the image of Sita haunted him day and night. He could not eat, sleep, or think of anything else.

He soon returned to Maricha's cave—this time, not with persuasion, but with threat.

"O Maricha," Ravana growled, "you warned me once, and I listened. But now I command you—become the golden deer, or I will kill you myself!"

Maricha stood silently. He was wise enough to know that death was now certain—either by Ravana's hand or by Ram's arrow. He closed his eyes and spoke solemnly, "It is better to die at the hands of Ram than to assist in this evil. I will do as you say."

Ravana smirked. His wicked plan had begun.

The next day, while Ram, Sita, and Lakshman were in the forest, Maricha used his magic to transform into a dazzling golden deer, with shining jewels on its horns and a glittering coat. He danced gracefully through the trees, catching Sita's eye.

"Look, Ram!" Sita cried. "What a beautiful deer! Please catch it for me."

Ram smiled. "Very well, Sita. Stay inside the cottage. Lakshman will guard you."

He picked up his bow and followed the magical deer deep into the woods. The deer would sometimes appear and then disappear. Realising that the deer was some kind of demon, Ram released an arrow that hit Maricha, who instantly fell down wounded.

Suddenly, Maricha let out a loud cry in Ram's voice: "Lakshman! Help me!"

Sita panicked. "Lakshman! Did you hear? Ram is in danger!

You must go!"

Lakshman was confused. "Sita, that is not Ram's real voice. He cannot be harmed. He told me to protect you."

But Sita, filled with fear, begged, wept and even blamed Lakshman for being callous. At last, Lakshman drew a shining line outside the cottage.

"This is the Lakshman Rekha," he said. "Do not cross this line, no matter what happens. You will be safe within it."

Then he left to find Ram.

And that's when Ravana arrived—disguised as a humble wandering sage.

"O Noble Lady," he said in a sweet voice, "I am tired and hungry. Please give me some food."

Sita, kind and gentle, brought food to offer him—but she could not cross the Lakshman Rekha. "Please come forward," she said.

Ravana's eyes gleamed. "I cannot," he lied. "It would be disrespectful."

Sita, thinking he was truly a sage, stepped just one foot across the line.

In that very moment, Ravana dropped his disguise! He grew tall, fierce, and terrifying. With ten heads and twenty arms, he grabbed Sita and rose into the sky in his flying chariot.

"Ram! Lakshman!" Sita cried, struggling in his grip. "Help me!"

The forest trembled. Birds flew in fear. Trees wept.

A mighty eagle named Jatayu, a friend of Ram's father, saw the crime and flew to save her. "Stop, Ravana!" he shouted. "How dare you steal another's wife!"

He fought bravely, clawing and biting and destroying Ravana's chariot. But Ravana, with his cruel sword, wounded Jatayu terribly and flew away with Sita, leaving the noble bird falling to the earth.

Sita's cries echoed through the skies, calling out to her Lord.

Ram had not yet returned… but the wind carried her voice to Him.

The time had come for the battle between light and darkness to begin.

24

RAM'S GRIEF AND THE NOBLE JATAYU

The golden deer was gone. Ram had struck it down with a powerful arrow, and in its final moment, Maricha had cried out in Ram's voice, tricking Sita and Lakshman.

Suddenly, Ram felt a chill in His heart. "That voice… It was not mine. It was a trap!"

He turned and ran back through the forest, faster than the wind.

At the same time, Lakshman came rushing toward Him.

"Brother!" Lakshman cried. "Forgive me. Sita heard that false cry and begged me to come."

Ram's eyes filled with worry. "Why did you leave her alone? I fear something terrible has happened."

The two brothers sprinted back to the cottage—but it was empty.

"Sita!" Ram called out. "Sita! Where are you?" He searched every corner, every tree, every path.

The birds were silent. The forest was still. There was no sign of her.

Ram fell to His knees, His voice trembling with sorrow. "My beloved Sita… Who has taken you from Me? What cruel heart has done this?"

Lakshman placed his hand gently on Ram's shoulder. "We will find her, brother. No power in this world can keep her hidden from You."

As they searched through the forest, they saw a trail of broken trees and crushed grass.

Following it, they came upon a noble and wounded bird lying under a tree. It was Jatayu, the mighty eagle who had tried to rescue Sita.

Ram rushed to him. "O Noble One! What has happened here? Do you know where Sita is?"

With great effort, Jatayu opened his eyes. His voice was weak but full of love. "O Ram… I saw the wicked Ravana… He took Sita and flew away in his chariot. I tried… I fought him… but he wounded me…"

Ram knelt beside him, His heart breaking. "O Jatayu, you are as dear to Me as My own father. You gave your life to protect My Sita. What greater hero is there?"

Tears fell from Ram's eyes as He gently held the great bird.

Jatayu smiled, his mission complete. "Now I can leave this world in peace… knowing I tried to serve You."

With those words, the noble Jatayu breathed his last.

Ram and Lakshman built a sacred pyre with their own hands and performed his final rites like sons would for a beloved father.

The flames rose, carrying the brave soul of Jatayu to the heavens.

That night, Ram stood under the stars, His face lit by the fire, His heart filled with grief and determination.

"Sita," He whispered, "wherever you are, I will find you. I will cross oceans, climb mountains, fight armies—until you are in My arms again."

The forest echoed His vow, and even the stars seemed to shine brighter, for the Lord of love and truth had begun His quest to rescue the queen of His heart.

25

THE SEARCH BEGINS—MEETING KABANDHA

After bidding farewell to the brave eagle Jatayu, Ram and Lakshman continued their journey through the dense forests of the south. The trees stood tall like watchful guardians, and the path ahead twisted through hills and wild lands.

Ram's eyes searched every corner. "Where are you, Sita?" His voice was soft, but His heart was strong.

They asked every tree, every stream, and every animal they passed. But no one had seen the demon king Ravana or his flying chariot.

Still, Ram did not give up.

Then one day, as they moved through a dark and gloomy forest, they heard a terrifying roar.

Suddenly, from behind the trees came a monstrous being! It had no head, a giant mouth on its stomach, and long, powerful arms that stretched across the forest.

It was Kabandha, a demon cursed into this strange and

frightening form.

He growled, "Who dares enter my forest? I will eat you both!"

He stretched out his enormous arms and grabbed Ram and Lakshman with a crushing grip!

But the two brothers remained calm.

With great skill and power, they drew their swords and in one swift move—chopped off both arms of the demon!

Kabandha fell to the ground, groaning in pain. But instead of roaring with anger, he began to transform.

Golden light surrounded him. His ugly form disappeared. Before their eyes stood a radiant, handsome being with a peaceful smile.

"I thank You, O Ram," Kabandha said. "Long ago, I was a celestial being, but a curse turned me into that terrible form. The curse would end only when Ram of Ayodhya would cut off my arms. You have freed me!"

Ram folded His hands. "Then tell Me, O Noble One, where shall I go to find My Sita?"

Kabandha's voice was full of wisdom. "Far south lies a mountain named Rishyamuka, near the Pampa Lake. There, You will meet a monkey king named Sugriva. He too has been wronged and is in hiding. Become his friend. He will help You find Sita. His warriors can search the earth, skies, and even the seas."

With that, Kabandha rose into the sky, shining like the sun, and disappeared into the heavens.

Ram turned to Lakshman, His eyes now filled with hope.

"The Lord never wastes anyone's suffering," He said softly. "Even this strange demon was part of our path."

And so, with the sky turning golden with the setting sun, Ram and Lakshman walked on—toward the Pampa Lake, toward their next friend, and one step closer to Sita.

26

MEETING SHABARI—THE DEVOTEE OF A LIFETIME

As Ram and Lakshman journeyed toward Mount Rishyamuka, the forests slowly began to glow with beauty once again. Birds chirped, the breeze was cool, and the flowers bloomed gently under their feet. It was as if the forest itself knew that the Lord of all hearts was coming.

Soon, they reached a peaceful and sacred place—a small cottage surrounded by trees, vines, and the scent of holy smoke. Here lived an elderly woman named Shabari, a humble devotee of Lord Ram.

She was no queen. She wore simple clothes made of bark. Her hut was made of leaves. But her heart was a shining palace of love for Ram.

Every single day for years, Shabari had swept the path, decorated the *ashram*, and plucked sweet fruits—waiting for the day her Lord would arrive.

The sages had told her, "One day, Lord Ram will come to bless you. Just wait with faith."

And so, she waited. Day after day. Month after month. Year

after year. And finally—that day had come.

As soon as she saw Ram and Lakshman entering her *ashram*, her eyes filled with tears. Her old hands trembled, and her heart beat like a young girl.

With great joy, she ran to greet them. Falling at their feet, she cried, "O Lord! My Ram! You have come! My life is now complete."

Ram gently lifted her and said, "Mother, I have come only because of your love. Your heart has drawn Me here."

She brought water to wash their feet, offered wildflowers, and then brought a plate of forest fruits she had lovingly collected.

But before offering them, she had tasted each one—just a tiny bite—to make sure they were sweet enough for her Lord.

Lakshman was surprised. "She tasted the fruits first?"

But Ram smiled with great love. "These are the sweetest fruits I have ever eaten. For they are offered with pure devotion."

Shabari's eyes filled with joy. "My Lord, I have no wealth, no palace, no learning. I only have love. Will that do?"

Ram replied, "It is more than enough. A heart filled with love is dearer to Me than all the gold and jewels in the world."

Then Shabari, in front of her Lord Ram, using her mystic powers, gave up her body. Attaining a celestial body, she rose to the heavens to be reunited with her *guru*.

And somewhere in the wind, even the trees whispered, *love alone is enough to touch God.*

27

RAM MEETS SUGRIVA, THE MONKEY KING

After blessing the humble and devoted Shabari, Ram and Lakshman walked toward Mount Rishyamuka, where destiny waited in the form of a monkey king named Sugriva.

High on the mountain cliffs, Sugriva lived in hiding. Once the powerful ruler of the Vanara (monkey) kingdom of Kishkindha, he had been unfairly driven out by his own brother, Vali. Now, with only a few loyal friends, Sugriva stayed far away, afraid and unsure of what to do.

But the moment he saw Ram and Lakshman walking at the foothills, tall and powerful with bows in hand, he was filled with fear.

“Who are these warriors in the forest?” he asked. “Have they come to harm me?”

He ordered his wise minister, Hanuman, to go speak to them and learn who they were.

Disguised as a humble mendicant, Hanuman leapt down from

the cliffs and landed before Ram and Lakshman with folded hands. His voice was sweet, and his words wise.

"O Noble Ones," he said, "you shine like the sun and moon. May I ask who you are, and what brings you to this forest?"

Ram smiled. He saw at once that Hanuman was no ordinary being—his devotion and intelligence glowed from within.

Ram gently replied, "I am Ram, son of King Dashrath of Ayodhya. This is My brother Lakshman. My wife Sita has been taken away by the demon Ravana, and I seek her across these forests."

Hanuman's heart leapt with joy. "Then your path and ours are meant to meet! My king Sugriva too has suffered unjustly. Perhaps you can help one another."

Hanuman lifted Ram and Lakshman in his arms and leapt high into the air—flying across trees and valleys—until they reached the top of Mount Rishyamuka.

There stood Sugriva, tall, strong, but full of sorrow.

Hanuman said, "Ram is no ordinary prince. He is the protector of *dharma* and has come as your friend."

Ram stepped forward with kind eyes and said, "Sugriva, I promise to help you win back your kingdom and defeat Vali. In return, help Me search for My beloved Sita."

Sugriva's eyes filled with tears. "Ram! I give You my word. My monkey army will search the corners of the earth to find Your Sita."

Then, before a sacred fire, the two made a vow of friendship. They walked around the flames, holding hands, promising loyalty, help, and brotherhood.

From that moment, Ram and Sugriva were more than allies—they were true friends.

And watching from nearby, Hanuman felt a deep joy rising in his heart. He knew that the time had come—for service, for courage, and for the greatest adventure of all.

28

VALI DEFEATED

The sun rose brightly over Mount Rishyamuka, and a new friendship had been born—between Ram, the prince of Ayodhya, and Sugriva, the exiled monkey king.

But to keep his promise and help Ram search for Sita, Sugriva had to first win back his kingdom from his powerful brother Vali, who had unfairly driven him away.

Vali was brave and immensely strong, but also proud and harsh in nature. Once, he chased a powerful demon named Mayavi into a cave to fight him. Before entering, he instructed his brother Sugriva to wait outside. A long time passed, and when Sugriva heard terrifying sounds and saw blood flowing from the cave, he feared that Vali had been killed.

Obeying his duty to protect the kingdom, Sugriva sealed the cave with a boulder and returned to Kishkindha, eventually becoming king.

However, Vali was not dead. He later emerged victorious and, seeing Sugriva ruling, assumed that his brother had betrayed him. Enraged, Vali forcefully drove Sugriva out, took back the throne, and even tried to kill him. Sugriva then fled to Rishyamuka mountain, where Vali could not go due to a curse.

Ram listened carefully and said, "Your pain is real, Sugriva. I will help you. You must challenge Vali to a duel. When he comes to fight, I will watch from a distance and protect you."

But when the day came, and the two monkey brothers began their battle, Ram did not shoot.

Why?

Because Sugriva and Vali looked exactly alike, and Ram did not want to strike the wrong one.

Sugriva returned, hurt and disappointed. "Ram," he said, "I trusted You… but You did not help."

Ram explained gently, "Forgive Me, friend. I could not tell you apart. But next time, wear this flower garland. Then I shall know it is you."

With fresh courage, Sugriva went again to challenge Vali.

This time, the battle shook the forest! Trees fell, rocks cracked, and the air filled with the roars of mighty warriors.

From behind a tree, Ram stood silently. When He clearly saw Sugriva—the one wearing the garland—locked in battle with Vali, He took out a single powerful arrow, strung His bow, and aimed with divine focus.

Twang! The arrow flew like a beam of light and struck Vali in the chest.

Vali fell to the ground, wounded. As he lay there, his anger faded, and he looked up at Ram.

"O Ram," Vali said, "why did You strike me while I was fighting someone else? You are known for Your righteousness."

Ram came forward and gently explained, "O Vali, you took what was not yours. You banished your brother unfairly and harmed the innocent. It is the duty of a king and a *kshatriya* to protect *dharma* and punish *adharma*."

Vali heard Ram's words and realised the truth. He folded his hands and said, "You are indeed the Lord of *dharma*. May my son Angada serve You well."

With those last words, Vali left his body.

Sugriva stood silently, his eyes full of emotion—not pride, but deep gratitude.

Soon after, the monkeys crowned Sugriva as the rightful king of Kishkindha, and he married Queen Tara, the widow of Vali. He promised to rule justly and to always remember Ram's help.

However, once he assumed the throne, Sugriva became immersed in royal pleasures and comfort. The monsoon rains arrived, and the search for Sita was postponed. Ram and Lakshman remained in a mountain cave on the Prasravana hill, enduring the rainy season in quiet patience.

But as the months passed, Sugriva forgot his promise.

At the end of the monsoon, Ram sent Lakshman to remind Sugriva of his vow. Angered by the delay, Lakshman stormed into the palace—but wise Tara intervened and calmed him.

Realising his mistake, a remorseful Sugriva bowed before Lakshman and immediately gathered his mighty monkey armies.

Turning to Ram, Sugriva declared, "Dear friend, forgive my delay. Now it is time. Let us begin the search for Sita."

And thus began one of the greatest searches the world had ever seen—across mountains, rivers, deserts, and even oceans—for the beloved queen of Ayodhya.

A search led by faith, fuelled by friendship, and destined to reveal the boundless power of devotion.

29

HANUMAN'S LEAP OF FAITH

The mighty monkey army had gathered. From every direction came thousands of monkeys—some could leap over hills, some could crush trees with their tails, and some could roar so loud that even lions ran away!

Sugriva divided the monkeys into four great teams and sent them in all directions to search for Sita.

"Look carefully," he said. "Ask birds, trees, sages, and rivers. Search caves and palaces. Do not return without news of the queen of Ayodhya."

The southern team was the strongest. It was led by the brave prince Angada and had the mighty Hanuman among them. Ram called Hanuman aside, looked into his eyes, and gave him a special gift—a precious ring from His finger.

"Give this to Sita," Ram said. "Tell her I am coming. She will know this ring can only come from Me."

Hanuman bowed deeply. "I will find her, my Lord," he promised.

The southern search army travelled far and wide. But days turned into weeks, and they still found no trace of Sita. The monkeys grew tired and hungry. Just when they were about to give up, they met a magical vulture named Sampati.

Sampati was the brother of Jatayu, the brave bird who had tried to stop Ravana when he kidnapped Sita. Sampati told them the truth: "Yes! I saw Ravana flying across the sky, carrying a crying princess. He took her to Lanka, his golden city across the great ocean."

Everyone rejoiced! However, their happiness quickly turned to worry. "Lanka is across the ocean," said Angada. "Who among us can leap that far?"

One monkey said, "I can jump ten *yojanas*." Another said, "Maybe twenty." But Lanka was hundreds of *yojanas* away!

Then, the wise bear Jambavan stepped forward and turned to Hanuman. He fixed his eyes with Hanuman's and made a tumultuous revelation.

"You, dear Hanuman, have forgotten who you are," he said. "You are the son of Vayu, the wind god. As a child, you tried to eat the sun, thinking it was a fruit! You are powerful beyond imagination. Now is the time to awaken that strength!"

Hearing these words, Hanuman's heart swelled with divine power. He stood tall, his form growing larger and brighter. The other monkeys cheered as he climbed a mountain peak, ready for the greatest leap the world had ever seen.

Standing on the mountain, Hanuman folded his hands and

prayed to Ram. "Let me find Mother Sita. Let this leap bring joy to my Lord."

Then—with one mighty roar—Hanuman leapt!

He soared through the sky like a shooting star. Mountains shook, clouds scattered, and sea creatures watched in wonder as the golden monkey raced above the waves.

Birds flew beside him. Winds carried him. Even the ocean rose up with respect, saying, "O Great One, may your journey be safe!"

After flying for hours, Hanuman saw a beautiful golden city on an island surrounded by glittering blue waters. It was Lanka, guarded by fierce demons and ruled by the mighty Ravana.

Hanuman hid in the trees as night fell.

"I must be clever," he thought. "This is not a place for noise or battle. I must search quietly."

With a humble heart and a brave spirit, Hanuman prepared to enter the city of Ravana—alone.

The search for Sita had truly begun.

30

HANUMAN ENTERS LANKA IN DISGUISE

Hanuman flew through the night sky and landed softly on the outskirts of Lanka, the golden city of Ravana. The whole city sparkled like the sun—its palaces shone with jewels, and tall towers touched the stars.

But Hanuman knew this was not a place for wonder—it was the home of the enemy. He shrunk himself very small, as tiny as a cat, and tiptoed into the city under the cover of darkness.

As he moved furtively from rooftop to rooftop, he saw terrifying demons—some with fangs, others with many heads, and some riding giant beasts. There were soldiers everywhere, guarding every corner of the city.

Suddenly, a powerful demoness named Lankini blocked his path.

"Stop! Who dares sneak into Lanka?"

Hanuman stood tall and said boldly, "I am a servant of Lord Ram. I've come in search of Sita!"

Lankini laughed. "No one enters this city without facing my strength!"

She rushed toward Hanuman—but with one gentle slap, he knocked her down. Surprisingly, Lankini arose and smiled.

"This was meant to happen," she admitted. "Long ago, Lord Brahma told me that when a monkey defeats me, it means Lanka's end is near. Go, great one. May your mission succeed."

With folded hands, she stepped aside.

Hanuman now searched from palace to palace, but he could not find Sita. He saw golden halls, silver gardens, and even Ravana sleeping with his many wives—but Sita was nowhere to be seen.

Hours passed.

Then, Hanuman saw a quiet, moonlit garden called Ashoka *Vana*. It was filled with fragrant trees, singing birds, and a gentle breeze. In the middle of this beautiful place sat a woman, dressed in a simple saffron cloth, her eyes filled with tears.

Hanuman's heart trembled in conviction. "It's her! It's Mother Sita!"

She looked thin and tired, her hair uncombed, and her face pale. But even in sorrow, she glowed like the moon.

Ravana had been trying to force Sita to marry him. He would threaten her, then try to charm her, but Sita always replied with firm words:

"I am the wife of Ram. You may have taken me by force, but you cannot touch my heart. My Lord will come for me."

Hanuman hid in the trees, waiting for the right moment.

When all was quiet, he softly dropped Ram's ring before her.

Startled, Sita looked around.

Then Hanuman appeared—still small and gentle, with folded hands. "Mother," he whispered, "do not be afraid. I am Hanuman, servant of Lord Ram. He has sent me to find you. Your sorrows will soon end!"

Tears rolled down Sita's cheeks—not of pain, but of hope.

She took the ring in her hands. "This is His… truly His…"

Hanuman bowed low. "Ram grieves for you every moment. He will come. I promise. But first, I must return and tell Him you are safe. Do you have a message for Him?"

With deep emotion, Sita said, "Tell my Lord I am holding on only for Him. Tell Him to come before it's too late, within one month. I cannot bear it any longer."

Hanuman promised, "Ram will come with Lakshman and armies of monkeys and bears. He will cross the ocean and defeat Ravana."

Before leaving, he gave Sita a token of Ram's strength—His faith, His love, and His vow.

But Hanuman's mission was not yet over. He wanted to gauge the enemy's power.

"Let them know," he thought, "that Ram's servant has come!"

And with that, he grew back to his giant form and began his heroic mischief.

31

LANKA ON FIRE

Hanuman had found Sita. He had given her Ram's ring and hope. Now, it was time to return and give Ram the joyful news.

But before leaving, Hanuman wanted to teach Ravana a lesson.

"I must shake this city," he thought, "so they know that Ram's servant has come—and His army is not far behind!"

So, what did he do?

Hanuman grew to a giant size once again and began leaping from palace to palace, destroying the royal gardens, uprooting trees, and roaring loudly. *"Jai Shri Ram!"* echoed through the skies.

Startled, Ravana sent his fiercest warriors to catch the mysterious monkey.

First came the mighty generals. Hanuman tossed them like twigs.

Then came Prince Akshaya Kumara, Ravana's own son. Brave

though he was, Hanuman defeated him in battle.

Ravana was furious. He turned to his most powerful son—Indrajit, the one who had defeated even gods. Indrajit used a magical weapon called the *Brahmastra*, which could not be escaped. Bound by his respect for Lord Brahma, Hanuman allowed himself to be captured, just to see Ravana face to face.

Chained and surrounded by guards, Hanuman was brought into Ravana's golden court.

There sat Ravana, the ten-headed king of Lanka, glowing with power and pride.

"Who are you, monkey?" he growled. "How dare you enter my city and destroy it?"

Hanuman smiled calmly and said, "I am the humble servant of Lord Ram, the prince of Ayodhya. I came to find His wife, Sita, whom you have stolen. Return her, or your entire kingdom will be destroyed."

The court fell silent.

Ravana roared in rage. "Kill him!"

But his wiser ministers stopped him. "He's just a messenger. You cannot kill a messenger—it is against royal *dharma*."

"Then burn his tail!" Ravana thundered. "Let him be mocked!"

The demons tied cloth soaked in oil around Hanuman's long tail and set it on fire.

But Hanuman just laughed.

He made himself gigantic again and leapt high into the sky—with his burning tail!

He jumped from rooftop to rooftop, setting fire to palace after palace. The golden city of Lanka was soon glowing not with wealth, but with flames. Smoke filled the skies. The demons screamed and ran in fear.

"Let this fire remind Ravana that Ram is coming!" Hanuman roared.

But just as he was about to leave, his heart remembered Sita.

"Oh no!" he gasped. "What if the fire reached Ashoka *Vana*?"

He quickly returned—but found Sita safe and protected by divine powers. Relieved, Hanuman bowed to her once more and said, "I will return soon, with your Lord."

Sita gave him her bejewelled hair ornament—as a sign for Ram.

"Give this to my Lord," she said, "and tell Him I await Him with every breath."

Hanuman took the ornament and leapt into the skies once more. He crossed the mighty ocean, the wind at his back, the waves below cheering his return.

He soon landed on Mount Mahendra, where the southern search army had been waiting—led by Angada, Jambavan, and the other monkeys. The monkeys ran to Hanuman, their eyes full of questions.

With a joyful smile, Hanuman raised the ornament in the air

and cried out, "I found her! Mother Sita is alive and waiting in Lanka!"

The monkeys danced, roared, and embraced one another. "Let's go! Let us give the news to King Sugriva and Ram at once!"

Together, they rushed through the forests, leaping over hills and rivers, until they reached Kishkindha.

When they arrived, Hanuman was brought into Ram's presence. He bowed deeply and offered Sita's ornament with both hands.

"My Lord," Hanuman said, "Mother Sita has been found. She is in Ashoka *Vana*, guarded day and night by demonesses. But she is alive, thinking only of You. She sends this to You… and her love."

Ram took the jewel in His hands. His fingers trembled. His eyes filled with tears.

He gazed at it as if it were Sita herself. "This… this is hers," He whispered, placing it against His forehead.

Then He turned to Hanuman and embraced him tightly.

"O Hanuman, you are dearer to Me than life itself. You have crossed the uncrossable. You have brought Me My soul."

Lakshman, Sugriva, and the entire monkey army rejoiced. The sky echoed with chants.

"Jai Shri Ram! Jai Hanuman!"

The time had come.

The Lord of Ayodhya would no longer wait. He would march to Lanka—not alone, but with millions of monkeys and bears, led by faith, fury, and friendship.

The rescue of Sita had begun.

32

THE BRIDGE OF DEVOTION

The forests of Kishkindha were filled with joy. Hanuman had returned with Sita's message, and the monkeys were dancing with excitement. Sugriva gathered his generals, and soon, a mighty army of monkeys and bears stood ready to follow Ram.

"Now begins the journey to Lanka!" declared Sugriva.

With Lakshman by His side, Ram led the army southward. Millions of monkeys marched—swinging from trees, leaping across hills, and chanting, *"Jai Shri Ram!"*

They crossed forests and rivers until they reached the southern tip of Bharat, a place called Setubandha, where the vast ocean stretched out endlessly.

There it was—Lanka, far across the water.

Ram stood silently at the seashore. The waves crashed before him, but He was calm. He prayed to the Ocean God (Samudra Deva) and sat in meditation.

For three days, Ram fasted and waited for the Ocean God to

appear and grant them a safe path. But the ocean remained silent and wild.

At last, Ram stood up and took His bow.

"I have been patient. But if you are unwilling to help, O Ocean, then I shall dry you up with My arrows!"

Ram's eyes flashed with divine fire. The sky darkened. His arrows blazed like lightning and struck the sea. The waves rose in terror.

Finally, the Ocean God appeared—glowing, humble, and afraid.

"O Lord Ram," he said, bowing, "I am bound by nature. I cannot dry up or become solid. But I will support a bridge. Let the mighty monkeys build it, and I will hold it up."

Ram smiled and lowered His bow.

Then, Sugriva ordered his engineers and heroes to begin.

The commander Nala, the son of the divine architect Vishwakarma, led the work. Under his direction, the monkeys began gathering mountains, boulders, trees, and even entire hilltops.

But something magical happened.

The monkeys began chanting *"Ram! Ram!"* and writing Ram's name on every stone—and mystically, the stones floated!

Yes, giant rocks floated on water—held up not by glue or ropes, but by faith and the holy name of the Lord.

Shoulder to shoulder, the monkeys formed chains, passing the stones to the ocean. Slowly, a path began to form across the waves.

|श्रीराम|
|श्रीराम|

Even the little creatures helped. A tiny squirrel rolled in the dust and dropped grains of sand onto the bridge. The monkeys laughed, but Ram smiled and gently stroked the squirrel's back with His fingers.

"Your devotion is as great as any mountain," He said.

Because of Ram's stroke, the squirrel gained three white stripes on its back—the mark of Ram's blessing.

Within five days, a magnificent bridge of floating stones stretched across the sea, sparkling under the sun like a ribbon of hope.

The army stood at the edge of the bridge, ready.

Ram turned to Hanuman and said, "Let us go. The time has come to end Ravana's cruelty and bring Sita back."

And with the ocean behind them and *dharma* in their hearts, the great army of Lord Ram began their march across the sea—step by step, stone by stone—toward the final battle between good and evil.

Finally, the army crossed the bridge. Monkeys, bears, and heroes—millions of them—set foot on the island of Lanka.

Ram looked across the land. "Sita, I am coming," He whispered.

Lanka had no idea what was coming—an army of devotion, led by the Lord of all worlds.

33

FINAL MESSAGE TO RAVANA

The mighty monkey army had crossed the ocean, walking proudly over the bridge they had built with devotion and teamwork. When they stepped onto the island of Lanka, their hearts were full of courage, and their minds were focused on one goal—to rescue Sita.

Ram, Lakshman, Sugriva, Hanuman, and all the monkeys marched forward until they reached a large forest called Suvela Mountain near Lanka. From the top of this hill, Ram could see the golden city far away, glittering like fire under the sun.

Ram's eyes grew soft. "Sita," He whispered, "I have come."

They made their camp there and rested before the great battle ahead.

Meanwhile, in Lanka, the sound of marching monkey feet echoed through the skies. Ravana heard the news.

"A huge army of monkeys has crossed the ocean!" said the guards. "They have reached Suvela Mountain!"

Ravana was surprised—and furious.

"Impossible! Who helped them cross the sea?" he roared.

To find out more, he called two *rakshasa* spies—Shuka and Sarana.

"Go and find out who these creatures are," Ravana commanded. "See what Ram is planning."

The two demons disguised themselves as monkeys and sneaked into Ram's camp.

But Hanuman, Jambavan, and the other sharp-eyed monkeys noticed them right away. With a roar, they captured the spies and dragged them before Sugriva.

"They are Ravana's men!" said Sugriva. "Let us punish them!"

But Ram stopped him. "No," He said calmly. "They are only messengers. Let them see our army, and let them return to tell Ravana that Ram has come."

The two spies were amazed by Ram's generosity and bravery. They bowed with respect and returned to Lanka.

Ram still hoped for peace over war.

He called Angada, the son of Vali, and said, "Go to Ravana's court and give him one last chance. Ask him to return Sita. If he agrees, there will be no war."

Angada crossed into Lanka and entered the golden palace fearlessly.

In front of all the demons, he stood tall and said, "I am Angada, son of Vali, and messenger of Ram! Return Sita to her Lord, and all will be forgiven. If you refuse, the earth will tremble from the wrath of Ram's arrows!"

Ravana laughed proudly. "I am the king of Lanka! I do not fear monkeys or men. Begone!"

Angada planted his foot firmly on the floor. "If any of you can move my foot, I will agree that Ram cannot win."

All the demons tried—but not one could move Angada's foot even a little!

Furious and embarrassed, they lunged at Angada—but he leapt high into the air and flew back to Ram's camp.

"They have refused, my Lord," he said. "They have chosen war."

Ram's face turned serious. He raised His bow and looked toward Lanka.

The time for words had ended.

It was now time for the arrows to speak.

34

VIBHISHANA CHOOSES RAM

In the golden city of Lanka, a storm of worry was rising.

Ravana had heard everything—the monkeys had built a floating bridge and crossed the ocean, and Ram was now camped just outside his city.

The *rakshasa* king called a meeting with his ministers and brothers.

"We must prepare for war!" he thundered.

But not everyone agreed. A gentle voice spoke up in the royal court—it was Vibhishana, Ravana's younger brother.

"Dear brother," he said humbly, "I beg you—return Sita to Ram. This is not our war. What you did was wrong. Ram is not an ordinary man—He is divine. If you do not surrender now, Lanka will fall."

But Ravana's eyes burned with pride. "You coward! You dare speak against me? Get out of my court before I destroy you!"

With a heavy heart but a clear mind, Vibhishana folded his

hands. "I have always served you, brother, but now I must serve *dharma*."

He rose from his seat, gathered four *rakshasa* companions, and flew across the sky—straight toward Ram's camp.

As soon as the monkeys saw five flying demons approaching, they became alarmed.

"Demons are coming!" shouted one. "Maybe it's a trick!"

Hanuman looked closely and said, "Wait... the one in front looks noble. His face is full of peace, not pride."

Vibhishana landed gently and folded his hands before Ram.

"My name is Vibhishana," he said with devotion. "I have left my wicked brother. I seek shelter at Your feet. Please accept me, O Ram."

But not everyone was sure.

Sugriva said, "My Lord, what if this is a trap? What if he spies for Ravana?"

Ram listened silently. Then He turned to His ministers and asked for their thoughts. Each one gave different opinions—some cautious, some hopeful.

Finally, Ram looked at all of them and spoke words so deep and beautiful that the trees, birds, and winds seemed to stop to listen.

He said: "One who surrenders to Me even once, saying, 'I am Yours,' I shall give protection, O Sugriva. This is My vow."

The whole camp fell silent.

Ram smiled gently and stretched out His arms.

"Vibhishana is now Mine. Let him be welcomed."

With joy, the monkeys brought water from the ocean and performed a small ceremony. Ram embraced Vibhishana and, right then, declared him the future king of Lanka.

Tears filled Vibhishana's eyes. "I have found my true refuge. My life has meaning now."

35

THE GREAT BATTLE BEGINS

With Vibhishana now on Ram's side, the camp was filled with hope and excitement.

Ram spoke kindly to him, "You know the ways of Lanka. Tell us how to prepare."

Vibhishana described the layout of the golden city, the strength of Ravana's army, and the names of his powerful warriors.

"Be ready," he said. "Lanka is filled with fierce demons—giants who can fly, become invisible, and use dark magic. But your victory is certain, because you stand for *dharma*."

Ram gave the order. It was time to move forward.

With conch shells blowing and war cries echoing through the forests, the monkey and bear armies marched from Suvela Mountain toward Lanka.

Ram and Lakshman walked at the centre, shining like the sun and moon. Sugriva, Hanuman, Jambavan, Angada, and millions of monkeys followed, carrying rocks, trees, and weapons.

When they reached the gates of Lanka, they halted and looked up.

The golden city stood tall with high walls, sharp towers, and iron gates. The *rakshasa* guards peered down, shocked to see the vast army of monkeys roaring like thunderclouds.

Ram now arranged the army in *vyuhas*—battle formations.

He placed the strongest monkeys at the front: Nala, Neela, Mainda, Dvivida, and Hanuman.

Lakshman stayed close to Sugriva. Jambavan guarded the rear.

Vibhishana stayed beside Ram and offered advice on the enemy's strategies.

Ram declared, "We do not attack the weak. Let us fight with honour. We have come to protect *dharma*, not to destroy without reason."

Meanwhile, inside the palace, Ravana stood on his watchtower and saw the enormous monkey army outside his city walls. He clenched his fists.

"Let them come! My warriors will crush them."

He called one of his brave generals, Shailusha, and ordered him to go out and attack the monkeys to test their strength.

Shailusha marched out with a battalion of demons, roaring fiercely.

But the monkeys were ready. A great battle broke out just outside the city.

The monkeys threw giant boulders and trees. The demons hurled sharp weapons and magical fire. The sky darkened with dust and the earth shook with the stomping of feet.

Neela, the monkey commander, faced Shailusha directly and fought him with amazing strength. With one powerful throw of a mountain, Neela smashed the *rakshasa* general to the ground.

The demons panicked and ran back inside the city.

The first victory belonged to Ram's army.

The war had truly begun. The monkeys roared in triumph.

Ram remained calm. "This is just the beginning," He said. "Many more battles lie ahead."

The sun began to set behind Lanka's towers. Both sides rested, knowing that the next day would bring even greater war.

36

KUMBHAKARNA AWAKENS

Monkey warriors and *rakshasa* soldiers clashed outside the golden gates of Lanka. But deep inside the palace, Ravana sat in silence. His heart was uneasy.

He had lost many generals already. His spies had failed. And Ram's army was only growing stronger.

Then he remembered his greatest weapon—his brother.

Not Indrajit. Not his magical warriors.

But Kumbhakarna—the mountain-like giant who slept for six months at a time, and when awake, was unstoppable.

"He is my last hope," Ravana thought. "If anyone can defeat Ram, it is Kumbhakarna."

But there was a problem. Kumbhakarna was asleep.

He had received a strange blessing from Lord Brahma: tremendous strength, but also a curse—he would sleep for six months and wake up only for one day.

That one day had come—but he was still snoring!

Ravana sent hundreds of soldiers to wake him up. They beat drums louder than thunder. They shook the ground with elephants. They roared into conch shells. They clapped, shouted, banged pots, and rang bells.

Still, Kumbhakarna did not move.

Then they brought in roasted meat, sweet drinks, and heaps of food. They waved it under his nose.

Sniff, sniff…

Suddenly—BOOM!

Kumbhakarna yawned so wide the palace shook.

He sat up slowly, rubbing his eyes. "Who dares wake me up?" he growled.

His soldiers bowed fearfully. "Your brother Ravana calls you. The city is under attack. A monkey army has crossed the ocean. The prince of Ayodhya has come to rescue Sita."

Kumbhakarna laughed.

"A monkey army? Ravana, what trouble have you brought now?"

He marched to the palace and stood before his brother.

"O Ravana," he said, "you took another man's wife. This is not *dharma*. You should have listened to Vibhishana. But now that war has begun, I will fight for you. After all, I am still your brother."

Ravana smiled. "You are my strength, dear brother. With you

on my side, I fear no one."

Kumbhakarna asked for food.

A thousand pots of rice, hundreds of buffalos, baskets of sweets, and jars of honey were brought for him. He ate everything in moments and roared, "I'm ready!"

He strapped on golden armour, picked up his massive mace, and began marching out of the palace like a walking mountain.

The earth trembled. The sky darkened. The monkeys atop Lanka's walls trembled when they saw him.

"Who is that?! He's bigger than an elephant! Bigger than ten elephants!"

Sugriva quickly ran to Ram. "My Lord, Kumbhakarna has come. He is the strongest of all *rakshasas*."

Ram remained calm. "Let him come. No matter how strong he is, *dharma* is stronger."

Hanuman and Angada gathered the monkey troops.

"Do not fear," Hanuman said. "We fight for Ram. Victory is ours!"

The sky echoed with chants.

"Jai Shri Ram! Jai Lakshman! Jai Hanuman!"

The battle between the giant and the army of faith was about to begin.

37

THE FALL OF KUMBHAKARNA

A sound like thunder echoed across Lanka.

Kumbhakarna, the mighty brother of Ravana, was awake—and marching to war.

His huge body looked like a walking mountain. His arms were as thick as trees. His eyes were glowing red. He carried a golden mace and wore armour that shone like the sun.

As he approached the battlefield, even the bravest monkeys felt fear.

"He's enormous!" cried one. "How can anyone fight him?"

But Hanuman roared, "Do not fear! We have Ram with us!"

With a terrifying roar, Kumbhakarna charged into the monkey army. He smashed trees and boulders with a single swing of his mace. He grabbed monkeys by the handful and threw them into the ocean. He crushed entire battalions under his feet.

Even great warriors like Neela, Dvivida, and Mainda were knocked back.

Blood flowed. Cries rang out. Dust rose like clouds.

The monkeys retreated and rushed to Ram. "My Lord," said Sugriva, "we tried our best, but Kumbhakarna is too strong."

Lakshman stepped forward. "Let me face him."

He shot many arrows that struck Kumbhakarna's arms and chest—but the giant laughed.

Next came Hanuman. He roared and hurled a mountain at the demon, but Kumbhakarna caught it and flung it back.

Hanuman fell but rose again, undaunted. However, even Hanuman's strength could not stop Kumbhakarna for long.

Then came silence.

Ram stepped forward, bow in hand, glowing like the rising sun.

Everyone stopped to look.

He spoke softly, "This is no ordinary enemy. But I will protect My people."

He strung His bow—*Sharnga*—and aimed divine arrows.

The battle of battles began.

Kumbhakarna charged like a storm. He threw trees and rocks, but Ram shattered them mid-air with His arrows.

Ram's arrows pierced Kumbhakarna's arms, legs, and chest. Blood poured out, yet the giant kept walking.

He grabbed a massive boulder and hurled it—but Ram split it

into dust before it could touch Him.

Ram now invoked powerful celestial weapons.

First, He used the *Indra-astra*, striking Kumbhakarna's legs.

Then the *Vayu-astra*, which cut off his arms.

Still, Kumbhakarna marched forward—without arms, without fear!

The monkeys watched in awe.

Finally, Ram invoked the *Brahmastra*, a divine arrow glowing with sacred fire.

He aimed at Kumbhakarna's chest and released it with great force.

Twang! The arrow raced like a comet and struck Kumbhakarna's heart, then sliced off his massive head.

With a sound like a mountain falling, Kumbhakarna crashed to the earth.

The battlefield trembled. The ocean roared. A mighty demon had fallen.

And the sky echoed with cries.

"Jai Shri Ram!"

38

INDRAJIT ENTERS

After Kumbhakarna's fall, the monkeys roared with joy. Ravana's mighty brother had been defeated by Ram Himself!

But inside Lanka's palace, Ravana burned with fury.

He turned to his eldest and most powerful son—Indrajit, also known as Meghnada.

"Go," he said. "Use your powers. Show them why even Indra, king of the heavens, fears you."

Indrajit bowed. He was a master of illusion, magic, and *astras* (divine weapons). He had once defeated even the heavenly gods.

Now, he was going to face Ram.

Indrajit entered the battlefield in a golden chariot, surrounded by *rakshasa* soldiers.

But then—he disappeared!

Using his *maya-shakti* (magical illusion), he became invisible.

The sky grew dark. Thunder rolled. Strange winds blew across the plain.

From the shadows, arrows rained down like fire. Monkeys screamed and scattered.

No one could see the attacker—but Ram and Lakshman stood firm.

Suddenly, Indrajit invoked a terrifying weapon—the *Naga-pasha*, a divine arrow made of enchanted serpents. He chanted secret *mantras* and released the weapon.

The snakes flew like lightning and wrapped themselves around Ram and Lakshman, binding them tightly.

They fell to the ground, completely paralysed.

The monkeys were shocked. "Ram! Lakshman!"

Hanuman rushed to them. Sugriva, Angada, and Jambavan stood protectively around their Lords.

"Who could do this?" asked Angada.

"It's Indrajit," said Jambavan. "He has vanished using dark magic. But don't lose hope. They are not dead. We must act quickly."

As the monkey army worried and cried, a divine light filled the sky.

The air turned cool and pure.

Suddenly, Garuda, the king of birds and mount of Lord

Vishnu, descended from the heavens.

With golden wings and blazing eyes, Garuda came closer to where Ram and Lakshman lay.

As soon as the snakes saw Garuda, they slithered away in fear—for Garuda is their eternal enemy!

The serpentine bonds vanished. Ram and Lakshman stood up, their strength and glow fully returned.

The monkeys danced with joy. "Our Lords are safe!"

Ram looked up at Garuda and offered a silent prayer. Garuda smiled, bowed, and returned to the sky.

Far away, Indrajit saw all of this with his magical sight. He was shocked.

"What power has saved them? How can they be free already?"

He knew now that this battle would not be easy. He disappeared again, planning his next dark attack.

39

LAKSHMAN INJURED

The battlefield was silent for a moment, as Ram and Lakshman stood recovered from the serpent weapon. The monkeys cheered, and Ravana's army trembled.

But far away, Indrajit was preparing again.

He knew he could not win through direct battle, so he turned once more to deceit and dark magic.

He entered a secret place called Nikumbhila, deep in the forest near Lanka, where he could perform a special *yajna*, a magical fire sacrifice that would make him invincible—but only if it remained undisturbed.

He began his rituals, chanting *mantras* and worshipping dark forces.

Vibhishana knew of this place and warned Ram. "If Indrajit completes this sacrifice, even the gods will not be able to defeat him. We must act fast."

Ram immediately sent Lakshman with Vibhishana, Hanuman,

and a group of strong monkeys to stop the sacrifice. They rushed through the forest and reached Nikumbhila just in time.

Indrajit saw them coming. Furious, he abandoned his sacrifice and leapt into battle.

The forest shook as the two forces clashed. Arrows flew like lightning. Hanuman and Angada fought bravely, but Indrajit was no ordinary warrior. He vanished again and reappeared, raining weapons from the sky.

Lakshman challenged him boldly. He raised his bow and shot sharp arrows that broke Indrajit's illusions. The two warriors fought like fire and thunder. The sky darkened with the force of their weapons.

Indrajit invoked powerful celestial weapons—*shaktis*, *Agni-astras*, and dark missiles. Finally, he released a terrible arrow charged with *maya* and venom.

It struck Lakshman in the chest with great force.

Lakshman fell.

The monkeys gasped. Hanuman caught him before he hit the ground. His breathing was faint. His body was still.

The army trembled.

"Lakshman has fallen!" the cries rang through the forest.

Ram heard the news and His heart nearly stopped.

"Lakshman…" He whispered. "If My brother dies, what use is

this life or this war to Me?"

The monkeys stood silently, not knowing what to say.

All looked to Hanuman, whose eyes were full of determination.

He looked at Jambavan, who said, "There is only one hope now. Sushena, the wise monkey physician, prescribes four life-restoring herbs. They are called Mritasanjivani, Vishalyakarani, Suvarnakarani, and Sanjivani. They grow in the northern Himalayas, on Mount Dronagiri. Bring them quickly before the night ends."

Hanuman folded his hands. "I will bring them. No matter what."

He bowed to Ram and leapt into the sky like a streak of fire, flying to the north—racing against time to save the life of Lakshman, the beloved brother of the Lord.

40

HANUMAN BRINGS THE MOUNTAIN

The wind whispered Hanuman's name. The stars moved aside to make way for him.

As he soared across oceans and valleys, over forests and cities, the trees below swayed in his path, and the clouds parted with reverence. Mountains bowed, and even the moon paused to watch.

After great speed and effort, Hanuman reached the mighty Himalayas. There, glowing like an emerald in the dark, stood Mount Dronagiri, covered in shining herbs. The entire mountain glowed with radiant lights—golden, blue, red, and green—each plant fragrant and alive with potency.

Hanuman searched carefully, but the herbs looked similar and he could not distinguish which were the ones Sushena had prescribed. He closed his eyes and prayed deeply to Lord Ram.

"With time running out," he said to himself, "and Lakshman's life in danger, I shall take the whole mountain."

With a powerful roar, Hanuman placed both hands on the

base of the peak. The ground trembled. Trees shook. Birds flew out in flocks. Deer ran in every direction. The mountain groaned—and rose.

With one mighty push, Hanuman lifted the entire mountain and placed it on his palm. The gods in the sky gasped. Carrying the mountain, Hanuman soared back through the night—shining like a second sun.

Back on the battlefield near Lanka, the monkey army waited. Their eyes were fixed on the sky.

Then, someone shouted, "Look! A light in the sky—it's Hanuman!"

The monkeys danced with joy. "He has returned! He has brought the mountain!"

Hanuman landed gently and placed the peak near Sushena.

Sushena quickly climbed up and found the four sacred herbs. He crushed them gently, mixed them into a healing paste, and placed the medicine on Lakshman's chest and nose.

Moments passed like eternity.

Then, Lakshman stirred.

His fingers twitched. His chest lifted. His eyes slowly opened.

He sat up straight, his strength fully restored, his face radiant like the sun rising after a storm.

Ram's heart overflowed. He embraced Lakshman tightly. "My dear brother," He said, "you are My very life. The light has returned to My world."

The monkeys danced and roared with joy.

"Jai Hanuman! Jai Lakshman! Jai Shri Ram!"

Hanuman, ever humble, once again lifted the peak and flew back to the Himalayas. He returned Mount Dronagiri to its rightful place, bowed to the herbs, and then came swiftly back to Ram's side.

He folded his hands and said, "Your servant has returned."

The army of Ram was now filled with new hope and courage.

The battle for *dharma* would continue—with Ram and Lakshman both standing strong once more.

41

THE DEATH OF INDRAJIT

The army of Ram rejoiced as Lakshman rose, alive and radiant.

But far away in Lanka, Ravana was struck with disbelief when he heard the news. His son, Indrajit, had used all his powers, his illusions, and his weapons, and still Lakshman lived.

Ravana's heart trembled.

Indrajit was enraged. His pride had been wounded. He returned once more to Nikumbhila, the sacred place where he had attempted his *yajna* earlier. He decided to perform the ritual again, for if completed without interruption, it would make him invincible in battle.

But Vibhishana understood his nephew's plan.

"O Ram," he said, "if Indrajit completes this *yajna*, even You will not be able to defeat him. He must be stopped now—before it is finished."

Ram turned to Lakshman. "You are the one chosen for this

task. Go with Vibhishana, Hanuman, and the mightiest of our army. End this once and for all."

With Ram's blessings, Lakshman set out for Nikumbhila. The jungle around the place was dark and eerie, filled with magical energy. Indrajit sat before the sacred fire, surrounded by weapons and incantations, invoking dark powers.

But before he could complete the final offering, Lakshman arrived. With a shout that shook the trees, he broke through the guards.

Indrajit stood up, his eyes glowing like fire. "You dare interrupt my ritual again? Then face your end."

He rose into the sky, showering arrows like rain. Lakshman countered with a stream of golden shafts, each guided by divine aim.

The two warriors clashed like thunderclouds. Indrajit used powerful weapons—*Agni-astra*, *Vayu-astra*, and weapons wrapped in illusion. But Lakshman, taught by Ram and trained by Vishwamitra and Vasistha, broke each one with perfect skill.

Hanuman and Vibhishana fought side by side, defeating Indrajit's allies and shielding Lakshman from surprise attacks. Vibhishana revealed secrets of Indrajit's tactics, helping to counter his invisible strikes.

Indrajit vanished from sight and attacked with dark *maya*. But Lakshman remained steady, his eyes closed, listening—not with his ears, but with the heart of a warrior guided by *dharma*.

Then Lakshman invoked the *Indra-astra*, a mighty weapon blessed by Indra himself. He strung it on his bow, prayed to Lord Narayana, and released it with great force.

The arrow sped through the sky like a comet. It pierced Indrajit's chest and broke through his armour of illusion.

With a scream that echoed through the forests, Indrajit fell—glorious in his fall, yet defeated.

The *rakshasa* army fled in fear.

Lakshman stood still, breathing heavy, bathed in light and glory. He had slain the undefeated son of Ravana—the one who had defeated even Indra, king of the heavenly gods.

Hanuman lifted him with joy. Vibhishana offered praise, and the monkey warriors chanted with thunderous delight.

"Lakshman ki Jai!"

The death of Indrajit was not just a victory of arms—it was a victory of devotion, discipline, and divine purpose.

Back at the camp, when Ram was apprised of Lakshman's triumph, He closed His eyes in gratitude. "Lakshman has upheld *dharma* once again," He said. "Now, only Ravana remains."

The tide of war had turned.

42

RAVANA ENTERS THE WAR

When the news of Indrajit's death reached the palace of Lanka, silence fell like a dark shadow. The *rakshasas* trembled. The queen Mandodari wept, and the sound of sorrow echoed through the golden halls.

Ravana sat still, unable to speak. His heart, filled with pride, now sank under the weight of loss.

Indrajit, his mighty son—the one who had defeated Indra himself, who could fight while invisible, who had bound Ram and Lakshman with serpent weapons—had been slain.

Tears welled up in Ravana's eyes. For a long time, he said nothing. Then, he rose from his throne and roared in a voice charged with fury, "Lakshman has taken my son. I shall take Ram's brother now."

With burning eyes and wild rage, he ordered his charioteer to bring forth his war chariot. Golden, wide as the sky, and drawn by swift black horses, it was armed with countless weapons.

He wore armour that shone like the sun, a crown upon his ten heads, and a bow that once belonged to Lord Shiva.

The *rakshasa* army rallied behind him. Ravana mounted his chariot, raised his bow, and rode out to the battlefield like a flaming mountain.

As he approached, the earth trembled. The sea roared. The sky darkened.

Ram saw the dust rising and said, "This is no ordinary warrior. It is Ravana himself."

Ravana did not wait. He rushed forward and began hurling arrows like thunderbolts. His arrows tore through trees and struck down many monkeys. Blood soaked the battlefield. His power was unmatched.

Ram sent Lakshman forward to face him.

The two warriors clashed. Lakshman fought with unmatched valour. He struck Ravana's bow, his horses, and his charioteer. But Ravana, mighty and terrible, released a fierce *shakti* weapon given by Shiva.

The weapon struck Lakshman in the chest and hurled him unconscious to the ground.

The monkeys gasped. Ram ran to His brother and lifted him in His arms. "O Lakshman! You are My very soul. You must not leave Me now."

Hanuman brought Sushena once again, who treated Lakshman with healing herbs. With time and care, Lakshman regained his breath. He sat up, weak but alive.

Ravana saw this and turned back toward Lanka, satisfied that Lakshman had been crushed.

But he did not know: Lakshman would rise again.

And soon, Ram Himself would enter the battlefield.

43

THE FINAL BATTLE

Ravana returned to the city of Lanka, thinking Lakshman was defeated. But when he heard that Lakshman had been revived by Sushena and was standing again, filled with strength, Ravana's fury burned brighter.

This time, he decided to end the war himself.

Climbing into his chariot once again, armed with divine weapons and fury in his heart, Ravana rode out onto the battlefield. He came roaring like a thundercloud, with his bow ready and ten heads held high.

Ram saw him coming and prepared to meet him. The monkeys cleared the field. The winds stopped. The sky dimmed. The earth waited.

Then, like two blazing suns rising at once, Ram and Ravana stood facing each other.

Each rode in a magnificent chariot.

Ravana's chariot was pulled by dark horses, wrapped in golden armour, and carried weapons from many worlds.

Ram stood on a chariot brought by Indra himself, sent by Matali, the charioteer of the gods. That divine chariot sparkled like the stars, with white horses and thunderous wheels.

The duel began.

Ram strung His bow and released a rain of arrows. Ravana countered with a storm of his own. The sky became dark with the force of their weapons. Arrows crashed mid-air. Fire met water, wind met earth.

Ravana roared and released weapons that had been given to him by Shiva, Brahma, and other celestials. He struck Ram's horses, Matali's hands, and even the wheels of the divine chariot.

Ram, calm and steady, invoked celestial *astras*. He countered every attack. His arrows split Ravana's bow, cut down his flags, and pierced each of his ten heads again and again—but they regrew instantly, by the power of the boons he had received.

The duel continued for a long time. Heavenly gods and sages watched from above, holding their breath.

Ram then invoked the *Brahmastra,* the supreme weapon blessed by Lord Brahma himself. It glowed with the fire of truth and the light of *dharma*.

Ram raised the arrow, prayed silently, and spoke: "If I have upheld truth, if I have lived by *dharma*, may this arrow strike down Ravana."

He released it.

The arrow blazed through the sky. It pierced Ravana's chest, shattered his heart, and carried him off his chariot to the ground.

The earth trembled. The sky cleared. A great silence fell.

Ravana, the king of Lanka, the terror of the three worlds, was dead.

The devas showered flowers upon Ram. The sages offered praise. The monkeys cried out with joy. Hanuman folded his hands in awe.

Ram stood silently, with His bow lowered.

The war was over.

44

RAM SENDS WORD TO SITA

Ravana, the mighty king of Lanka, now lay on the battlefield, defeated by the arrow of Ram. His ten heads, once proud and fierce, had fallen still. The battlefield was quiet. The gods in the sky rejoiced. The earth sighed with relief.

Vibhishana stood near, gazing at his fallen brother. Though Ravana had walked the path of *adharma*, he had once been a great devotee of Lord Shiva and the protector of Lanka. Vibhishana's heart was torn between duty and grief.

Ram turned to him and said, "Though your brother acted unjustly, he was a warrior and a king. Perform his funeral rites with honour. That is your *dharma* as his brother and a devotee of righteousness."

At first, Vibhishana refused. "He brought this upon himself by his wickedness. How can I perform the last rites of one who stood against *dharma*?"

But Ram replied with deep compassion, "He was brave. He fought like a true *kshatriya*. Now that he has fallen in battle, he

is no longer an enemy. It is the law of *dharma* to honour the dead. Let not hatred remain in your heart."

Vibhishana bowed his head. "You are *dharma* itself, O Ram." Then, with help from the other *rakshasas*, he performed the last rites of Ravana with fire, water, and sacred *mantras*.

Meanwhile, the queens of Lanka, led by Mandodari, arrived at the battlefield. Seeing her husband's lifeless body, Mandodari wept. "O Lord of Lanka, you were wise, learned, and mighty. But blinded by desire, you brought ruin to yourself and to us all."

She lamented deeply, but also acknowledged the greatness of Ram. "This must be Narayana Himself," she said. "No ordinary man could have defeated you, O Ravana."

After the cremation, Vibhishana returned to Ram and bowed at His feet.

Ram said, "You are now the rightful king of Lanka. Rule with compassion and *dharma*. Protect your people."

The monkeys and bears placed a golden crown on Vibhishana's head. The drums of Lanka sounded, not in fear, but in a new beginning.

Then Ram looked to Hanuman.

"Dear Hanuman," He said, "You have always been My messenger, My servant, and My friend. Now go to Ashoka *Vana* and give Sita the news: her sorrow is over. Tell her that I am well, Lakshman lives, and the enemy is no more."

Hanuman bowed with folded hands. His eyes filled with emotion. “It shall be done, my Lord,” he said, and leapt into the air.

The sky opened once more for the son of the wind.

45

THE MESSAGE OF JOY

Far away, in the silent garden of Ashoka trees, Sita sat beneath a flowering tree. Her eyes were closed, but tears still slipped down her cheeks.

The battle sounds had stopped. The air was still. Yet her heart trembled.

"Has my Ram survived? Is Lakshman safe? Has the war ended?"

Suddenly, the soft rustle of leaves reached her ears. She looked up.

From the sky descended Hanuman, glowing like the morning sun, his heart overflowing with joy.

He landed gently before her, folded his hands, and said with a smile that lit the garden:

"Mother Sita! The dark clouds have passed. The sun has risen. Ram has won. Ravana has been defeated. You are free!"

For a moment, Sita just stared at him. The words were too sweet, too grand to believe.

"Ram… lives?" she whispered.

"Yes," said Hanuman, bowing low. "Not only does He live, but He has conquered all evil. Lakshman too is well. And Ram Himself has sent me to give you this message: your sorrow is over."

Sita's hands trembled. Her lips parted. Her tears flowed, but this time, they were not of pain—but of joy.

She raised her eyes to the sky and whispered, "O Ram… after all the darkness, You have come."

Hanuman's eyes too filled with emotion.

"Shall I destroy these cruel *rakshasis* who tormented you?" he asked, his voice fierce.

But Sita, full of compassion, said softly, "No, my child. They were only doing their duty. Let no more hatred remain. Let peace return to Lanka."

Hanuman folded his hands again. "Mother, please prepare yourself. Ram will soon call for you. The time of reunion has come."

Then, with a heart as light as the clouds in spring, Hanuman leapt back into the sky to return to his Lord.

Behind him, in the Ashoka grove, flowers bloomed brighter, and birds sang sweeter—because Sita's heart had been touched by hope once more.

The garden, once filled with sorrow, now overflowed with light.

The Lord of Ayodhya and His queen would soon meet again.

46

THE REUNION AND RETURN TO AYODHYA

The war had ended. The cries had fallen silent. The ashes of battle rested on the ground, and in the heart of Lanka, a soft wind blew—carrying with it peace.

Ram stood calm and radiant, like the sun after a long storm.

He turned to Vibhishana and said, "Please bring Sita to Me."

Vibhishana humbly bowed and went to Ashoka *Vana*. With utmost respect, he brought Sita, now bathed, adorned in simple yet elegant cloth, her heart steady and full of longing.

As she approached, all the monkeys and bears lowered their heads. Even the heavenly gods in the sky waited silently.

Sita bowed before Ram, her eyes full of love.

But Ram, though moved, stood firm.

He said in a steady voice, "I have fulfilled My duty as a *kshatriya*. I have destroyed the enemy and rescued you from captivity. But, O Sita, you have lived in the house of another man. The world may doubt your purity. And I must answer to *dharma*."

A silence deeper than the ocean followed.

Sita's eyes filled with tears—not from hurt, but from the sorrow of being misunderstood.

But she did not speak in anger. With folded hands, she said calmly, "O Ram, if my mind, body, and soul have remained fixed only on You, may the fire witness my truth."

She turned to Lakshman and said, "Build me a pyre."

The monkeys wept. Even the gods gasped.

But Lakshman, with trembling hands, built the fire.

Sita walked toward it with fearless grace. She bowed to the flames and stepped inside.

But just then, the fire blazed golden, then blue, and then—out of it rose Agni-deva, the heavenly god of fire, carrying Sita in his arms.

He said, "O Ram, Sita is pure. No evil touched her. I myself protected her in the fire of Lanka. She is spotless, loyal, and devoted to You alone."

Ram's face softened. His eyes glistened.

He stepped forward and took Sita into His arms. "I never doubted you," He whispered. "But it was necessary to prove to the world what I already knew."

The heavenly gods rejoiced. The skies rained flowers. The sun shone brighter.

Then, Indra and Brahma appeared before Ram and said, "You

are no ordinary man. You are the Supreme Lord—Narayana Himself. You have come to uphold *dharma*."

But Ram smiled humbly. "I am a son of Dashrath, bound to his command. I walk this path for his sake, and for the sake of *dharma*."

The heavenly gods were moved beyond words.

Soon after, Vibhishana brought the magical Pushpaka Vimana, the flying chariot of Ravana, and offered it to Ram.

"Return to Ayodhya, O Lord," he said. "Your people await You."

Ram smiled. With Sita beside Him, and Lakshman, Hanuman, and the monkeys boarding the divine chariot, they soared into the sky.

As they flew northward, Ram pointed to each place they passed—Kishkindha, Rishyamuka, Chitrakuta, the hermitages of sages, the banks of sacred rivers.

And then—Ayodhya.

The city was blooming with joy, cleaned and decorated with lamps and flowers.

Ram looked at Hanuman and said, "Go ahead to Ayodhya. Tell Bharat that we are coming."

Hanuman bowed joyfully and flew through the sky like the wind.

He reached Nandigram and found Bharat sitting in meditation, holding Ram's sandals on the throne.

"O Bharat!" Hanuman cried. "Your Ram is returning!"

Tears flowed from Bharat's eyes. "Is it true? My brother is coming back?"

He leapt up, ringing bells, calling ministers, decorating the streets.

"Prepare the city! Let every home shine with joy! Ram is coming home!"

When the Lord arrived, Bharat ran forward and fell at His feet. Ram lifted him and embraced him tightly. "O Bharat," He said, "you kept the kingdom safe with such love and purity. You are truly the crown jewel of our family."

Ram then entered the city with Sita and Lakshman. The people cried with joy.

Children danced. Drums rolled, conches blew, flowers rained from balconies. The elders blessed them. The whole city looked like a sky full of stars.

Ram had returned.

Bharat placed the royal sandals back on Ram's feet. The brothers embraced. The queen mothers wept and laughed together.

And then, in a grand ceremony, Ram was crowned king of Ayodhya, seated on a golden throne beside Sita.

Lakshman stood by His side, and Hanuman, ever humble, sat near His feet.

The world rejoiced. Truth had won. *Dharma* had triumphed.

The exile had ended. And love had returned to the hearts of all.

The streets echoed with chants. "*Jai Shri Ram!* Victory to Ram!"

And thus, began the most beautiful time in the world's history—*Ram Rajya*—the golden rule of truth, kindness, and peace.

No one went hungry. No one told lies. Rain came on time, and the world lived in harmony.

Because the Lord of *dharma*, the king of kings, had come home.

47

THE GLORY OF RAM RAJYA

As Lord Ram ruled, the people of Ayodhya cheered and celebrated, for a new era had begun.

It was not just the rule of a king.

It was the rule of righteousness.

The age of truth, love, and peace.

It was the beginning of *Ram Rajya*—the most glorious time on Earth.

Under Ram's rule:

- The skies gave perfect rain.
- The Earth gave rich harvests.
- The rivers flowed clear and full.
- There was no hunger, no disease, and no sorrow.
- No one ever told a lie.
- No one hurt another.
- Parents were respected, teachers were honoured, and even animals lived without fear.

Sita was the ideal queen—wise, kind, and full of grace. She cared for the women of the kingdom like a gentle mother.

Lakshman served Ram day and night, never resting, always standing by his brother's side with love and devotion.

Bharat ruled the people with justice and care, as if Ram's heart beat in his chest.

Shatrughna protected the borders and built cities, bringing peace wherever he went.

Children grew up learning about *dharma*. Elders were cared for like treasures. And every morning, the city echoed with the chanting of Ram's name. The sages rejoiced. The heavenly gods smiled.

And even the animals of the forest knew—they were safe.

People from distant lands came to see this golden kingdom, and they would say in wonder: "In Ayodhya, even the wind seems to sing Ram's name."

Ram ruled for thousands of years, with no pride, only compassion.

He taught by example—showing the world that true greatness is not in power, but in service and truth.

Even today, the story of Ram, Sita, Lakshman, Hanuman, and their divine journey is sung across the world—in temples, in homes, in hearts.

And whenever the world forgets what is good and right, someone whispers the sacred words:

"Remember Ram."

Because His story is not just from the past—it is forever.

Thus ends the sacred story of the *Ramayana*—where truth wins, love shines, and *dharma* walks the Earth.

ABOUT THE AUTHOR

Nityanand Charan Das, an esteemed spiritual counsellor and practicing monk for the past 18 years at ISKCON Chowpatty, Mumbai, is a disciple of the world-renowned spiritual leader, philanthropist, and best-selling author, His Holiness Radhanath Swami.

A celebrated author of several national bestsellers, Nityanand Charan Das has captivated readers with works such as A Monk's Almanac, Icons of Grace, and Ask the Monk. His latest book, SHIVA, also has joined the ranks of national bestsellers, offering a profound exploration of the hidden dimensions of Lord Shiva and providing deeper insights into His unexplored persona.

Among his other notable works are Bound by Love, Vedic Tales, and Epic Tales of Wisdom, each reflecting his unique ability to blend timeless wisdom with contemporary relevance.

Deeply committed to enriching urban lives, Nityanand Charan Das aims to help individuals lead lives of purpose, fulfilment, and satisfaction, both professionally and personally. Specializing in mentoring today's youth—children, teenagers, and young professionals—he inspires them to reconnect with their roots and embrace a simpler, happier life.

As a sought-after speaker, he travels extensively worldwide, delivering enlightening discourses on ancient wisdom of the Bhagavad Gita, Shrimad Bhagavatam, Ramayana, and Mahabharata in a manner that resonates with audiences of all ages. His discourses are heard in multiple countries across the globe.

Born into an army family, his early ambition was to join the armed forces. However, through Krishna's divine orchestration, he did not clear the NDA interview despite excelling in his group. This led him to pursue Mechanical Engineering, eventually finding his true calling as a monk at the age of 24.

Over the years, Nityanand Charan Das has served in various capacities, including deity worship, organizing festivals and pilgrimages, and leading vibrant kirtans. Through his outreach, he has nurtured a flourishing spiritual community in Mumbai, across India, and internationally.

His message is simple yet profound:

"Spiritual Life is not a life of Rejection.

It is a life of Connection"

We don't need to give up anything; we only need to embrace this valuable dimension to enrich our lives.